The Buzz about *This Is Not The Career I Ordered…*

"Any woman interested in reinventing her career should read this book. Caroline Dowd-Higgins is a breath of fresh air. Her practical steps to reinventing your career will show you how and in a way to move forward."

—Debra Fine, bes  *Small Talk he Big Talk*

"Most of us will have seven to ves, so how to recharge, reignite and reinvent ourselves is something *everyone* needs to know. And, if you're lucky enough to already have the career you ordered, you should read this book because it will definitely ensure your success!"

—Peggy Klaus, Executive Coach and author of *BRAG! The Art of Tooting Your Own Horn Without Blowing It* and *The Hard Truth About Soft Skills: Workplace Lessons Smart People Wish They'd Learned Sooner*

"Landing a job is one thing; finding personal and professional fulfillment through working your passion is another entirely. *This Is Not the Career I Ordered* is a must-read for anyone who has not yet found that 'sweet spot' in their career. It is a friendly, easy read, but not at all simplistic, with valuable insights for first-job seekers through seasoned professionals."

—Kathryn Marion author of: *GRADS: TAKE CHARGE of Your First Year After College!*

"Caroline Dowd-Higgins challenges us to find careers we are passionate about and provides the practical tools, resources and strategies to do just that. The book is full of real life engaging success stories that we can all learn from and be inspired by."

—Ruth Stergiou, CEO Invent Your Future Enterprises

"Caroline Dowd-Higgins captures the essence of entrepreneurship – fearless authenticity, crazy creativity and radical reinvention. Sitting down to read *This Is Not the Career I Ordered* is like listening to 20 amazing mentors share the secrets of their success. Whether you are contemplating a reinvention or whether you are already in the middle of one, there is no reason to do it alone – let the women in this book inspire you, push you and give you the strength to take the next step."

—Starla Sireno, Founder, CEO Fearless Women Network

"Extraordinarily relevant, on-point, and thoughtful message for individuals in any stage of their career journey. Working closely with college students of all ages, I shall certainly recommend this book to them and to our alumni."

—Julia M. McNamara, PhD, President Albertus Magnus College, New Haven, Connecticut

"Wonderfully written and easy to read, Caroline Dowd-Higgins', *This Is Not the Career I Ordered*, prepares women for career change with anecdotes, concrete suggestions and superbly informational web sites highlighting many new products and services. For women in the medical, or any field contemplating a career change, this book is a must have resource and a great gift for friends, family, and colleagues. The stories of women who are successfully recharging, reigniting and reinventing their careers prove the adage 'If you love your job you never work a day in your life'."

—Dr. Kathleen Toomey, Medical Director of The Steeplechase Cancer Center at Somerset Medical Center – New Jersey, and a Medical Oncologist in Private Practice

"Career success in the second decade of the 21st century belongs to those who courageously move beyond the boundaries of their comfort zones toward exploration of possibilities. Dowd-Higgins masterfully weaves together anecdotes of women who have done precisely this with solid tools and tips for parlaying who you are into what you can become."

—Lois P. Frankel, Ph.D., author of *Nice Girls Don't Get the Corner Office* and *See Jane Lead*

"This much needed book provides practical advice and action steps to recharge an existing career or execute a major career reinvention. The inspiring stories of women who are thriving in their new careers, many as entrepreneurs, provides insightful wisdom that is just as applicable to men. Caroline Dowd-Higgins captures the essence of finding passion inspiration in our work that leads to ultimate career satisfaction."

—Dr. Donald F. Kuratko, *The Jack M. Gill Chair of Entrepreneurship Professor of Entrepreneurship & Executive Director* Johnson Center for Entrepreneurship & Innovation at the Kelley School of Business, Indiana University - Bloomington

"STOP THE PRESSES!!! Caroline Dowd-Higgins' book: *This Is Not the Career I Ordered* is a HIT! Everything you want to know and more in this authentic, revealing, funny, inspiring book. With practical career advice, who doesn't want to move forward in their careers! Let's order seconds on this book."

—Sallie Felton, Life Coach/Transition Specialist, International Talk Radio Host

THIS IS
NOT THE
CAREER
I ORDERED

THIS IS
NOT THE
CAREER
I ORDERED

*Empowering
Strategies from
Women Who
Recharged,
Reignited, and
Reinvented
Their Careers*

CAROLINE DOWD-HIGGINS

REINVENTION PRESS
BLOOMINGTON, INDIANA

Published by
Reinvention Press
P.O. Box 6043
Bloomington, IN 47407

ISBN: 978-0-9827318-0-2

Edited by: Deborah C. Stephens
Copy editor: Karen Kibler
Text and cover design by Mayapriya Long, Bookwrights

Printed in the United States of America

"You've got to follow your passion. You've got to figure out what it is you love—who you really are. And have the courage to do that. I believe that the only courage anybody ever needs is the courage to follow your own dream."

—Oprah Winfrey

CONTENTS

Acknowledgements

I am indebted to the many women who shared their amazing stories for my book and blog project. Their contributions have changed my life, inspired me with hope, and solidified my belief that great things happen when women come together in community. Thank you for sharing your trials and tribulations as well as your triumphs – we can all learn from your journeys.

This book would never have happened if it wasn't for Deborah C. Stephens. She empowered me with this opportunity and took a risk on a new author. Throughout the process she has been an amazing mentor, editor, and friend, and for her I am truly grateful.

To the fabulous Stacey J. Miller, my publicist extraordinaire, whose constant support and enthusiasm is palpable and motivating. Kudos to Steve Bennett and his team from Author Bytes, who created my blog and website. Special thanks to Mayapriya Long of Bookwrights, who designed the cover and interior of the book and to Karen Kibler for her copy editing expertise.

To my friends and colleagues, Nichole Williams and Beth Kreitl who were originally slated to be coauthors on this project: I truly appreciate your feedback, support, and unending enthusiasm. I am so proud of both of you for prioritizing your values when your lives were taking new and exciting turns. I look forward to another book so that we can collaborate the next time around.

I want to acknowledge my family for their patience and understanding during the creative process. To my husband, C. David Higgins, who taught me to be ready when opportunity knocks and serves as my constant inspiration. To my parents, Marty and Nancy Dowd, who provided unconditional support as their opera-singing daughter reinvented herself, and for believing in me and this project. To my sister, Jennifer Bruner, who patiently read through many drafts and shared my book and blog news with her vast network. To my brother, Thomas Dowd, who was willing to let me impart my career development wisdom on him as he took the next steps on his professional journey.

To the many friends and colleagues who have touched this project in a variety of ways: Mrim Boutla, Julia McNamara, Amy Hume, Frank Kimball, Chelsea Sanders, Rachel Seed, Kim Conley, Kathryn Marion, Ilona Hajdu, Paul Marrangoni and my Grateful Divas: Rebecca Keith, Jennifer Heichelbech, Melissa Korzec, and Joni McGary.

And to the myriad of people who are not on this list but helped in so many ways – thank you!

PREFACE

I came to this book project by an unexpected route. A friend of mine heard a fabulous speaker at a women's event and called to tell me about her. She said the speaker and author, Deborah C. Stephens, recently relocated from California to Indiana and was looking to build her network of women in the Midwest. I reached out to Deborah and set up a lunch meeting and we've been friends ever since.

To my great fortune, Deborah has become one of my mentors. She is part of my resource team and the catalyst for this book. She coauthored the women's book: *This Is Not the Life I Ordered* (one of her eight bestselling books) and was looking for experts to pen additional books with the *This Is Not The* (fill in the blank) *I Ordered* theme. She quickly encouraged me to write *This Is Not the Career I Ordered* because of my passion and expertise in the career development arena.

The two-year journey started at Deborah's kitchen table much like the gatherings with friends she describes in her women's book. I began interviewing women I knew who had experienced a career transition. In the spirit of great networking, these women connected me to their friends, colleagues, and family members who also had stories to share. Within a year, I had spoken with over 150 women in the USA, Canada, and England as a result of national press inquiries and good old-fashioned relationship building. That number is still growing as my career transition blog www.notthecareeriordered.com which built a foundation for this book, is still going strong.

Survival Guide

Since I have experienced my own career transition and reinvention, I have a personal stake in this project. I was inspired by the women I interviewed and their commitment to helping others learn from their experiences, to make your journey a little less rocky. The power of women in community is extraordinary.

While the career advice and action steps I present are applicable to men as well, the book is told through the eyes of women, who have become stronger and more confident in their quest for reinvention. You will laugh and cry and be motivated by their experiences, but most importantly, you will learn from these women.

My goal is to provide you with a survival guide in the form of a *Reinvention Toolbox* that shows you how to implement your own personal career reinvention. Some readers will want to recharge, or reignite an existing career while others will pursue a major overhaul. The action steps for success are in this book.

Empowerment

Working in a university setting for a decade, helping students and alumni forge their personal career paths, has been a rewarding experience for me. My private practice and public speaking engagements have also given me opportunities to work with amazing people around the country. But the most gratifying moment for me is when a student or client begins to walk tall with a renewed self-confidence and the ability to own their strengths and articulate their passions and values. That is true empowerment and the ultimate message of this book.

Think of this book as your personal career development journal. Take notes on the pages and fill out the exercises right in the book, so that you have a resource to refer to later. Some of the steps in the *Reinvention Toolbox* require self-reflection, time, and planning but many are quick how-to steps to energize you and get you started on your path to reinvention now. The wisdom at the end of each individual woman's story, and each chapter, is a wealth of information – all of which can help you take a step forward on the journey to achieving your goals.

Pay-it-Forward

Think about the other women in your life (mothers, daughters, sisters, friends, etc.) who can learn from the resources assembled by the women showcased in this book. I hope you will join me in sharing the generational wisdom with others so that we can support each other and serve as champions for those struggling to find peace, happiness, and prosperity in a career.

We all know that these are difficult economic times and that the employment landscape has been devastated. The reality is that you may have to stay in your current job for a while to make ends meet or until you land the new position that better matches your values, interests, personality, and skills. That's okay – my goal is to help you get started on this journey of reinvention so that when the time is right, you'll be ready!

Tap into the power and enthusiasm of the sisterhood and enjoy the steps in creating a new you – one that is recharged, reignited, reinvented, and ready to take the world by storm. Women in community are amazing – enjoy the journey!

1

LEARN TO SING A NEW TUNE

1. TRADING STAGES: FROM OPERA SINGER TO CAREER COACH

Performing is like oxygen for me – I love the energy of a live audience and honed my talents to become an opera singer. I was a professional Diva – the good kind that is, since there is no room for inflated ego or bad attitude in the ultra competitive musical job arena. I enjoyed the intellectual stimulation as well: mastering foreign languages, embracing new cultures, and being a savvy self-promoter and negotiator. My musical career took off and I was living my dream.

Over the course of several years, the lack of financial security, benefits, and living the life of the proverbial starving artist was taking its toll, financially and emotionally. It takes a lot of money to sustain a career in the opera world since the voice lessons, musical coaching, and accompanist fees are a constant part of keeping yourself fit and at-the-ready for the next gig. Additionally there is the long distance travel for auditions, being away for months at a time, and the reality of missing my husband who was back at home. So, I knew I needed more in my life to make it complete; but how does an opera Diva with degrees in music find a new career?

What's a Diva to Do?

I would be remiss if I didn't own up to the fact that my personal career reinvention journey was an emotional and difficult one. I went through the full gamut of emotions from fear to rage when my career did not go as I had planned. I couldn't figure out what I was doing wrong until I finally realized that I wasn't doing anything wrong – perhaps this just wasn't the best fit. That epiphany did not come easily or quickly so my goal is to help make your career transition a smoother one.

You're Not in Kansas Anymore, Dorothy!

As I looked back, I realized that I was the type of kid that was incredibly focused at a young age. I fell in love early with performing, and developed the requisite thick skin, honed my craft, and earned an undergraduate and Master's degree in music to complete my package as a professional singer.

I paid my dues with blood, sweat, and tears, and in my mind I was destined for a glamorous life as a performing artist who would enjoy the jet setting travel and perhaps even taste a modicum of fame. When I took off my rose-colored glasses, I realized that truly living the artistic life was not what I expected. Even though I still loved performing, continuous travel became exhausting, as did living in hotels and billeted rooms in the homes of Opera Company board members. I was lonely.

Perseverance or Denial?

The life of a performing artist for me was feast or famine and while the feasts were delicious, the famines were extremely debilitating emotionally. While I did achieve recognition and earned accolades for the work I was performing, deep down I knew something was missing. For far too long, performer's guilt kept me from admitting what I was missing. I forged ahead, trying to convince myself that my next big break would bring the recognition and solvent lifestyle I really wanted. I was not about to give up – that went against every fiber of my being. I was bound and determined to make this work, come hell or high water.

Looking back, I realize that I was ignoring the red lights in my way, not seeing them as signs that I was possibly on the wrong path. I was always taught to persevere and a performer has to suffer for her art, right? **Let me tell you very clearly that nobody has to suffer for his/her career.** You should be joyful in your work and once I came to terms with that notion, my entire world opened up.

Giving Up Guilt

After some serious soul searching, I realized that singing opera was something I did but it did not entirely define who I was as a person. That was liberating, but how was I going to make a living? Last time I looked, opera singers were not high on the list of sought-after nonmusical job candidates. Or so I thought....

Now, years after my personal career reinvention, I consider myself Jill-of-all-Trades since I have enjoyed a myriad of career opportunities in television, radio, and theatre using my voice and stage presence professionally. My career repertoire also includes event planning, marketing and communication, public speaking, employer development, recruiting, and career counseling. Now I can add author, journalist, and blogger to that list and I am confident that I will continue to add experiences that play to my strengths since I am empowered with the knowledge that I can do many things well.

A Grateful Diva

I am still performing, but now I don't have the stress of earning my living as a singer. I founded a professional singing group, *The Grateful Divas*, with fellow singer friends and I perform solo and ensemble shows to raise money for nonprofit and charitable organizations nationally. I'm now a Diva on a philanthropic mission and I have been liberated to enjoy myself as a musician in ways I never thought possible.

Currently, I have the great privilege of serving as a Director of Career and Professional Development at the Indiana University Maurer School of Law. I am coaching the next generation of lawyers to be ready for the prime time realities of the world-of-work. I also have a vibrant career consulting practice and speak nationally on career and professional development issues. In addition to my career reinvention blog, I also write career columns for the *Huffington Post* online and *The Chronicle* newspaper.

I truly believe that anyone can learn to sing a new tune and have proven it true in my own life. Taking what I have learned on a personal level, and with the myriad of clients I have worked with, I have created a navigational system for career change and reinvention. In this book, I will introduce you to amazing women from around the world and a variety of job fields who have mastered the art of change by recharging, reigniting, and reinventing their lives and their careers.

2.   CAREER REINVENTION IS AN ART

In this tumultuous economy, many women have been forced to reinvent themselves due to downsizing and workforce cutbacks. Others have realized that their careers did not honor their values and they were on a live-to-work carousel and could not get off. We have a *new normal* in our present day career world with unemployment numbers higher than they were during the Great Depression, so I know how scary a career transition can be at this time. My goal is to empower you with strategies and action steps so that you can make career choices that suit your unique situation.

I have interviewed over 150 women across the globe for this project and several of their stories appear in this book. If you enjoy learning about how other women have reinvented themselves, many of these stories are featured on my blog, www.notthecareeriordered. com. After talking with so many women, I was relieved to know that many of them also struggled with the guilt of giving up one career to pursue another, especially if their education or training supported the original career. I can tell you from experience, it's a scary step to take; but once you let go of the guilt, it will be very liberating and eventually, confidence-building.

The Reinvention Journey

We all have a myriad of transferable skills that we can utilize for a variety of careers regardless of our educational backgrounds. Heidi Roizen, one of the women I interviewed, shared that a career is like a marathon over the course of a woman's life. It's rare that we have the same career for the entire journey so consider new opportunities that match your passion as you travel the personal mile markers in your life.

Career reinvention is truly an art, one that you alone control. Nobody can reinvent you, except you. It is a powerful concept and one that I hope will bring you self-confidence once you learn more about the steps and strategies to help you move forward towards your individual goals.

3.   BEGIN WITH WHAT YOU VALUE

Choosing the women to feature in this book was a difficult task since I truly cherish each woman's unique story. I picked the stories for the book to showcase a variety of career fields and diverse experiences amongst the women. These ladies shared their hopes and dreams as well as failures and emotional journeys so that you could learn from their experiences. Amazing things happen when women come together in community and now you are part of the strong contingent of women who are contemplating, or have undergone, a career change. These women are a resource you can turn to for advice and inspiration and they personify the power of the sisterhood.

The first step in a career reinvention is to get quiet with your SELF and assess your **values, interests, personality,** and **skills**. In career development jargon, we call these VIPS. First, we'll focus on **values**. A thoughtful self-reflection can help you determine your plan of action for a career transition. We all know people who are unhappy in their jobs. So take the time to thoughtfully consider what you value because **research shows that values are the biggest predictor of career satisfaction.**

You Alone Can Identify Your Values

We each value different things and there are no judgments about which are better or worse. You are in control of what you value as well as how you pursue new opportunities that match your passion.

Some people value variety, autonomy, security, prestige, or flexibility in the workplace – the options are endless. Think about what motivates you and why.

- What are your peak experiences?
- How do you spend discretionary money?
- Whom do you admire?
- What reasons have driven your past decisions?

Being aware of what you value in your life is important because a career choice that is in line with your core beliefs and values is more likely to be a lasting and positive choice.

Values – Palooza!

My values epiphany came when I realized that I value security in my work. I was an emotional wreck when I worked from audition to audition, not knowing where my next paycheck was coming from. I also value variety which is why I work many different jobs as a consultant, writer, public speaker, university director, etc., which make up my comprehensive career picture. When I was able to recognize what I valued and what I was missing in my performance career, I could move forward with a plan for my new career possibilities.

Here is a brief list to get you started thinking about what you value. Remember, the values possibilities are endless.

Take the time to consider your top values based on what you want in your life now. Values change as we progress through life so what you value now may be completely different from a career you had in the past. I talk with many women who leave and re-enter the workforce before or after they have children, or take care of elderly parents. This is a great example of how your values can change with different circumstances in your life.

Write it Down!

I encourage you to utilize this book as a personal career development journal where you can start to map out your values and take additional notes as I guide you on your unique career discovery journey. You will begin to connect the dots and see a clearer picture of what is important to you so that you can pursue a career path that's right for you.

SAMPLE VALUES

Intrinsic Values

Achievement	Equality	Power
Balance	Giving to Community	Respect
Belonging	Honesty	Responsibility
Commitment	Independence	Self-Respect
Contributing	Influence	Spirituality
Environmental Awareness	Integrity	Status

Work Environment Values

Aesthetics	Flexible	Quiet
Autonomy	High Earnings	Relaxed
Benefits	Learning	Sense of Community
Comfortable Income	Location	Structured
Excitement	Personal Safety	Time Freedom
Fast-Paced	Predictable	Security

Work Content Values

Adventuresome	Decision-Making	Physical
Advocacy	Detailed	Problem-Solving
Analytical	Helping	Public Contact
Challenging	Initiating	Research
Conceptualizing	Leading-Edge	Risk-Taking
Creative	Organizing	Variety

Work Relationship Values

Caring	Harmony	Open Communication
Competition	Individualism	Recognition
Cooperation	Leadership	Support
Diversity	Loyalty	Teamwork
Friendships	Management	Trust

From the values list, circle at least one (the more the better!) career value in each of the four main categories: **Intrinsic Values**, **Work Environment Values**, **Work Content Values** and **Work Relationship Values**. Take some time to think about why these are important to you and how you can fit them into your career plan. Eventually, you will rank them in order of priority so you can refer to this when you have done a full values, interests, personality, and skills (VIPS) self-assessment.

It's rare to find a career that meets all of your values all the time. But having an awareness of what you value will help you look for, or create, new opportunities that are gratifying. Having an accurate understanding of what you value will help you answer the question: Why should I engage in *this* line of work?

Honor Your Values

Values mean different things to different people so be sure to honor what **you** value in this self-reflection process. If I queried five of my clients who identified the same value of *financial success* and asked them to define it they would each articulate very different answers, and that's a good thing! You alone can determine what you value, so put your blinders on and tune out the advice of well-meaning family and friends for the purpose of this exercise. Really consider what would satisfy **you** in a career.

From the time I was a little girl, I remember my grandfather talking about the importance of finding a job with good benefits. He worked his entire career at General Motors and valued the healthcare and retirement benefits from that company. Before I was old enough to work, I had absorbed my grandfather's career values by family osmosis. I caution you to discover what is important to you so that you are not steered off your personal values course by outside sources. Take the time to make your own values decisions. While I have great respect for my grandfather, over time and with serious self-reflection, I was able to identify my unique career values. I discovered that although we shared the *benefits* value, my complete values list, and how I ranked *benefits*, was much different from that in his viewpoint.

Think about the jobs you have disliked during your career and reflect on the values that were not being met in those situations. This may help you find harmony in a future career opportunity and give you a better understanding about why values predict satisfaction at work.

4. FIND WHAT MAKES YOU TICK

Now that you have an understanding of what values are and how they drive your career gratification, you can begin to explore how you can match your values to a potential job. The next predictor in your personal self-assessment is **Interests.** Knowing your interests can help you discover your passion and give you clarity about choosing a career. **Interests are the biggest predictors in career selection since we gravitate towards doing what we like.**

One of my favorite assessment tools is the **Strong Interest Inventory® (Strong)** which measures career and leisure interests. Working with a career development professional who is certified to administer and interpret your Strong assessment results can help give you clarity about how your interests impact your career choices.

The Strong tool breaks interests down into six categories:

Realistic – (Doers) People who have athletic or mechanical ability, prefer to work with objects, machines, tools, plants, or animals – or to be outdoors.

Investigative – (Thinkers) People who like to observe, learn, investigate, analyze, evaluate, or solve problems.

Artistic – (Creators) People who have artistic, innovating or intuitional abilities, and like to work in unstructured situations using their imagination or creativity.

Social – (Helpers) People who like to work with people – to inform, enlighten, help, train, develop or cure them, or are skilled with words.

Enterprising – (Persuaders) People who like to work with people influencing, persuading, performing or leading, or managing for organizational goals or for economic gain.

Conventional – (Organizers) People who like to work with data, have clerical or numerical ability, carry things out in detail, or follow through on others' instructions.

There is No Magic Bullet

While assessments are not meant to give you all the answers and identify perfect career options, these tried-and-true career development industry tools can take you on a deeper guided self-reflection than you might be able to do by yourself.

When I discovered that my Strong code was SAE – Social, Artistic, and Enterprising, it confirmed my love for all things creative, but gave me a new awareness about my interest in helping people. It also identified my interest in persuading and influencing others and helped me discover how I could *perform* in a different way on the job.

I remember fondly a client of mine who worked in the television industry. After a year working at a national affiliate TV station, she came to me because she was unhappy working the news beat and considered changing fields altogether. I encouraged her to think about what she loved about her job as well as what she disliked. It turned out that the news beat was not a good match but the day-to-day tasks at the station in her capacity as a producer still gratified her. After an interests self-reflection exercise she articulated that she loved food, cooking, and products related to the culinary industry. If only she could find work that celebrated her interests.

Rediscover Your Interests

We began to look at ways to match her interests to her skills in telecommunications and eventually discovered that she could marry both in a career. She now works for a Food Network TV program as a producer and is thrilled to go to work every day because her foodie-loving interests are being met.

Keep in mind that your interests may indeed lead to a career opportunity. Why not rediscover what really interests you and begin to look for, or develop, career opportunities in this arena? Here are some action steps to get you started:

- Make a list of your interests (past, present, and a future wish list) and be ready to add to this inventory as you continue with your career self-reflection.
    - ✧ Consider these interest sources, the possibilities are endless:

✓ TV shows, movies, books you read for pleasure, news papers, magazines, etc.

✓ Classes you take for fun, volunteer work, sports, arts, community activities, etc.

✓ Websites or blogs you frequent, things you do when not working, family activities, etc.

What are the patterns you see with your interests? Are there ideas you have about a dream job and how you could incorporate your interests into a career? Remember that your interests change over time so perhaps you are craving a new career opportunity that speaks to your current interests. Keep adding to your interests log and be sure to update it as your interests change. Career development is a journey and you may have many different occupational chapters during your work life.

If the Strong Interest Inventory® is appealing to you, I can help you find resources available in your geographic area to take this assessment. I can also guide you on a customized interest self-discovery so feel free to contact me at www.carolinedowdhiggins.com.

5.   WHY PERSONALITY MATTERS

Following the career development steps of self-evaluating your VIPS (values, interests, personality, and skills) it's time to focus on personality. This happens to be one of my favorite parts of the career reinvention and self-reflection journey. Personality refers to your unique patterns of mental, emotional, physical, and behavioral characteristics.

You may have heard of the **Myers-Briggs Personality Type Indicator™ (MBTI)**, an assessment tool that breaks personality down to four preferences.

- Where do you draw your energy? Do you prefer to focus on the external world of people and actions or are you energized by ideas and feelings of the inner world?

- How do you perceive information? Do you focus on the realities of the present or the possibilities of the future?

- How do you make decisions? Are you guided by objective, analytical reasoning or subjective, personal values?

- What is your need for order in life? Do you prefer to be organized and planned or spontaneous and flexible?

Your personality preferences play a big role in the type of work you may like or dislike. Very often I'll work with clients who wish they could be doing someone else's job in their organization because their position is simply not a good fit.

Channel Your Personality

My MBTI assessment shows that I am an extrovert as one of my four preferences. I am energized by people so I'm happiest in my work environment when I am working with, or presenting to, groups of people. A flashback to my performance days – clearly, I still love an audience! Introverts might enjoy working in smaller groups or one-on-one with people, since their batteries are recharged when they spend time alone. Personality plays a huge role in how you interact and communicate with people in your work environment.

A former colleague of mine thought she had landed the perfect new dream job that enabled her to work from home. Quickly she became lonely in her home office and missed interacting with people on a regular basis. She needed stimulation and variety from interacting with people to be gratified in her work environment. She is now in a similar job but is working in an organization outside of the home, where she comes in contact with people every day. This is a much better match for her personality.

Know Thy Self and honor your inborn personality type to help you find a career that matches your natural tendencies. There are many fabulous career coaches certified to administer and interpret the MBTI, but I caution you to find experienced practitioners who can guide you through this exciting self-reflection. The unofficial online versions cannot give you the full picture of the instrument and how personality plays a role in your career world. Take the time to find someone with credentials, or contact me via my website www.carolinedowdhiggins.com, and I can assist you.

The MBTI now has expanded versions (Step II and Step III) that delve even more deeply into additional competencies and personality traits that may help you further discover your ideal career fit.

6.   LEARN FROM THE QUEEN OF TRANSFERABLE SKILLS

My Diva training has actually served me well in all my career endeavors. When I first contemplated a career change, I was paralyzed with fear because I didn't think I was marketable in any other field. My degrees were in music – how was I going to convince an employer that I had other assets to make me a value-add in an organization! In the beginning, I didn't own the various skills in my professional toolbox and took for granted the fact that I was a skilled communicator, writer, marketer, and promoter since these were competencies I employed regularly and easily for my singing gigs.

I also learned the importance of my stage presence and realized that when I spoke, people listened. My trained singing voice translated well into a compelling speaking voice and I was able to get people's attention and keep it by using my voice in a different way. My multicultural awareness, knowledge of foreign languages, and travel savvy also helped me connect with people and relate to diverse constituents. I had a plethora of skills I never showcased consciously and it was exciting to learn how to articulate these with prospective employers.

The Power of my Voice

Every day I speak with students and private clients who have no real sense of what their skills are. Simply put, a skill is an ability, based on training or experience, to do something well. We all have skills and the trick is to discover what they are and market them with humble confidence to make ourselves attractive to employers (and beyond) so that we can utilize these skills in the workplace and in life.

As a trained opera singer turned Career and Professional Development Coach, I like to think of myself as the Queen of Transferable Skills. When I was making my unique career transition, most employers were very dubious about what I had to offer. In time, I became my own best advocate and was able to market to others what I did well. Over the years, I have worked with thousands of students and clients who have studied everything from Creative Writing to Analytical Chemistry and when they own the transferable skills in their profes-

sional toolbox, they understand how degrees and credentials are significant, but only play a part of their overall package in the job market.

I guarantee that you have hidden skills you have not yet owned
and embraced. Once you discover your skills you can start to connect
the dots with your other VIPS (values, interests and personality) and
find opportunities that are a true match for you career-wise.

Skills Treasure Hunt

Since it can be hard to consider your skills alone, I urge you to ask
people in your circle of trust (family, friends, and colleagues) to share
what they think you do well. Having others help identify your skills
can be very powerful, but ultimately you are in control over which
skills you choose to market on your new career path.

Ask five trusted individuals who know you well to write down a
list of skills they believe you possess. It's best to give them some lead
time so they can give serious thought to your unique skill set. Having
multiple written lists will allow you to compare what others believe
you do well with the list you develop about your own skills. See if you
can detect a pattern among the lists.

To get you started, skills fall into three main categories:

Transferable Skills – these can be taken from job to job and
are important in many career sectors. Examples include: communication (verbal and written), critical thinking, analysis,
leadership, and project management.

Specialized Knowledge – these are skills relevant to a particular job or career field. Examples include: operating labora-
tory equipment, computer program proficiency, French Cui-
sine cooking, and foreign language fluency.

Adaptive Skills – these are personal attributes you bring to
the professional environment and often the most sought-after
by employers. Examples include: motivation, initiative, integrity, flexibility, resilience, and self-management.

Here is a list of sample skills. Take the time to consider what skills
are in your toolbox, as well as those you may want to develop. Circle
all the skills on the list that you believe you have now. Identify skills
you want to develop with a different mark. Use a third notation to

indicate the skills you love to use – those that give you strength.

Reflect on multiple skills that show up in the individual categories: **Communication Skills, Humanitarian Skills, Physical Skills, Creative Expression, Mental/Creative, Mental/Analytical,** and **Leadership/Management** to determine if your skills cluster in a particular area.

SAMPLE SKILLS

Communication Skills		
Facilitate Groups	Speak Before Groups	Explain
Sell	Interview	Meet the Public
Influence/Persuade	Consult	Promote
Serve as Liaison	Write	Motivate
Humanitarian Skills		
Take Care of Others	Listen	Coach
Provide Hospitality	Advocate	Counsel
Train	Instruct	
Physical Skills		
Use Body Coordination	Operate Equipment	Repair/Restore
Work Outdoors	Hand Dexterity	Build/Construct
Creative Expression		
Produce Events	Food Production	Perform
Compose/Author	Display	Craft-making
Invent	Design	Create Images
Mental/Creative		
Use of Memory	Synthesize	Conceptualize
Visualize	Use Intuition	Demonstrate Foresight
Improvise	Brainstorm	
Mental/Analytical		
Budget	Manage Records	Evaluate
Calculate	Solve Problems	Analyze
Observe	Monitor	Research
Categorize	Edit	Compute
Leadership/Management		
Mediate	Implement	Supervise
Negotiate	Coordinate	Initiate
Organize	Plan	Determine Policy
Delegate	Decision-Making	Follow Through

Rediscovering what you do well can be an exciting journey. Since most jobs require utilizing these skills at least 40 hours per week, you want to make sure that you are employing skills you enjoy that also give you strength.

The VIPS discovery process is very empowering, and positively influences your decisions and actions on the path to finding a great career fit. Awareness about your values will bring you satisfaction. Refining your interests will lead you to a career that is gratifying. Learning about your personality will help you to make occupational choices that suit your preferences. Owning the skills that give you strength will allow you to market yourself as a valuable commodity in the world-of-work.

2

Utilize the Power of the Women in Your Backyard

7. These are Not the Careers They Ordered

The research for this book began two years ago when my mentor introduced me to this project. The world was entering a *perfect career storm* as people were being let go from long-term jobs and dissatisfaction at work was at an all-time high. I set out to interview women who made a transition from one career to another with the hopes of helping others who were considering a move and to provide them with sound advice and action steps.

To date, I have interviewed over 150 women across the USA, Canada, and England. Women came out of the woodwork to answer press inquiries and they shared their wisdom in order to help you learn from their mistakes, as well as their successes. The network is alive and well and almost every woman with whom I spoke recommended another amazing woman from her personal set of contacts that was ideal for this project.

I spoke with women from all walks of life from entry level twenty-somethings to a woman in her 80s who feels too young to retire. Some changed careers because they were forced to do so after a downsizing or lay-off. Others were looking for new challenges and opportunities to really play to their strengths. Many tapped into their entrepreneurial spirit and embraced an opportunity to be their own boss while others had experienced burn-out or illness from a job that was debilitating.

The Only Thing Constant is Change

Not every change was from a negative work environment. Some of these women sought new ways to stimulate and challenge themselves. Many found innovative opportunities after retooling or seeking additional credentials to empower themselves with more focused skill sets.

The common denominator in all the women I interviewed is that they took matters into their own hands and became their own change agents. It was scary, exhilarating, challenging, and gratifying, running the full gamut of emotions. But in the end – all these women are happy that they pursued a change.

Life is too short to be miserable or unsatisfied at work. We spend the greater part of our waking hours on the job, so I want you to find work that gives you an opportunity to thrive. How you function at work plays a significant role in your happiness at home. My goal is to help you recharge, reignite, and reinvent your career so that you can lead a more satisfying life.

Since in this book I was not able to showcase all the incredible women I interviewed, I continue on my career transition blog (www. notthecareeriordered.com) to celebrate the many women I have met during the process of writing the book. Do check out this site as a continuing resource for career and professional development strategies and inspiration.

8.   Inspiration to Pay-it-Forward

One of the most gratifying things about interviewing all the women for this book was the realization that they wanted to help others learn from their personal journeys. Many have incorporated a give-back plan in their work environments and others are committed to paying-it-forward and helping others as mentors and advisors.

Throughout my life, I have been fortunate to have mentors who have provided me with expert guidance and I am so pleased to share with you what I have learned. Women are nurturers and I encourage you to look to the women in your life and discover how you can cultivate them. I guarantee that they will reciprocate and support you someday when you are in need.

Career Karma

I believe it takes a village to develop a career in the professional world and the first step is to surround yourself with people you respect and trust. The next step is to be conscious of how you can pay-it-forward and help others in return. We introduce new relationships into our lives every day whether consciously or not, and having the awareness that you can help others is not only good for the karmic circle of life, it's just the right thing to do.

Angela Jia Kim, my very first book interviewee, is CEO and Founder of **Om Aroma & Co.** and Co-Founder of **Savor the Success. com**. She has built her businesses on the *Give, Give, Get* rule when networking. Nothing is more of a turn-off than someone who is in it just for themselves. When you are a genuine networker and operate from a position of authenticity, people are more apt to help you. After all, business is all about human interaction, so considering how you can help others will increase your personal capital.

Paying-it-forward is not just applicable to networking. Whether it is volunteering your time and expertise or donating a percentage of targeted proceeds towards a worthy cause, generosity and the spirit of community are being celebrated on a grand scale.

It's Not the Destination but the Journey

Careers are a lifelong journey and we've all had people that were instrumental in helping us along the way in good times and in bad. Make an effort to be conscious about how you are helping others because what goes around really does come around. It may require a new mindset, behavior, and strategy, but at the most basic level, all it requires is that you make a choice. By giving back, you just might be a role model for someone else and help make the pay-it-forward conduct become the norm for everyone.

9. BUILD YOUR PERSONAL BOARD OF DIRECTORS

It's no secret that a mentor can be a terrific resource as you navigate your personal career path. Some organizations assign mentors; other relationships develop naturally when like-minded people hit it off. If you are your own boss, or don't have a company to connect you with a mentor, you can and should pursue mentors on your own.

Seeking a mentor starts simply with asking for advice from a trusted professional who has *been there and done that* in your desired industry. Start by asking for information and advice and see how the relationship develops. You will know when you have made an authentic connection with someone and taken the relationship beyond colleague to personal guru.

Mentors help to improve upon your strengths and guide you along your path to success, providing inspiration and resources that come from experience. A mentor can also help you set and accomplish your goals. Mentors will guide you and offer practical ideas about how you might do things differently. We all need at least one mentor who can speak candidly and offer constructive criticism, even when we don't want to hear it.

Build Your Personal Resource Team

Mentors should help boost your self-confidence and empower you to achieve and overcome obstacles. But don't think that you need one perfect mentor to help you on your professional way. In reality, life is full of mentors that can advise you day by day, sharing important bits of wisdom incrementally over time. I encourage you to take a close look at the many people in your life and reflect on how they may actually be mentoring you right now. Build your own personal Board of Directors, your personal posse to guide you in your career pursuits.

You can gain a wealth of support and resources with a team. Sometimes these relationships develop organically and sometimes you need to take the driver's seat and ask others for help. No matter which, mentors volunteer their time and experience, so always show them your respect. Listen, don't argue – and always follow up with a personal thank-you note or gesture of gratitude. The mentor relation-ship is powerful and valuable, so cultivate it wisely and be mindful of how you can help others and keep the circle of wisdom continuous by becoming a mentor yourself.

I know that many of you reading this book will make a connection to at least one woman who has been showcased. I urge you to reach out to these women and incorporate them into your personal resource team. They understand the power of positive relationships and have all benefitted from the guidance of others. At the end of their stories in each chapter, they provide valuable resources which they utilized during their career transition that may be advantageous to you.

10. UNLOCK YOUR PASSION

A recurring bit of career advice from the women with whom I con-ducted interviews across the globe was to *find your passion*. It sounds simple but I am shocked at how few people are actually in tune with their personal passions. I'm not talking about romance; rather, I'm asking you to consider what motivates and inspires you on a regular basis and how you can incorporate this into your career.

In his book, *The One Thing You Need to Know About Great Man-aging, Leading and Sustained Individual Success*, Marcus Buckingham shared a statistic:

"Only twenty percent of people report that they are in a role where they have the chance to do what they do best every day, and the rest of the world feels like their strengths are not being called upon every day."

The operative word is *role* – those in the rest of the eighty percent are not mediocre or incompetent, they are just not in the right role. I challenge you to consider what gives you strength and by doing so, discover your passion.

How Do I Find My Passion?

First you need to understand what passion in this context means. Passion can be expressed as a feeling of excitement, enthusiasm, or compelling emotion towards something. A person is said to have a passion for something when she has a strong positive affinity for it. In the career world, passion is something for which you are extremely enthusiastic and can imagine pursuing as a vocation without calling it *work*.

Answer these questions to help discover your possible career passions:

- What do you love to do in your free time?
- What are the skills that come naturally to you without much thought or effort?
- If you had no limitations (financial, education, location, etc.) and could do any job, what would you choose?
- What types of things energize you?
- What activities, subjects, or causes have you been deeply involved with?
- What are some areas in which your family and friends consider you an expert?
- When you are online, or at a bookstore, what subjects most appeal to you?
- Do you possess deeply held beliefs for which you have a calling in life?
- What are the types of things that people ask you for help with?
- What are some of the big goals you want to achieve in life?

I have always been passionate about public speaking. Perhaps it's part of my performance gene. I am energized by opportunities to teach or present to groups where I can tap into my enthusiasm for commanding an audience. My passion has been monetized by presenting at conferences nationally and by giving workshops in corporate environments and seminars for my students at Indiana Law. When I am speaking to a group of people and engaging them in a conversation about a special topic, time flies for me and it never feels like work. My goal is to create more opportunities to play to my passions and to deliver messages that help people own their strengths and self-confidence in the workplace.

By adding your passions to your self-assessment results you will begin to see what you are best at, what you enjoy most, and what areas of advice and expertise people seek from you. You can now begin researching careers that honor your passions and your VIPS.

Who is in Your Circle of Trust?

A small step in owning your strengths is to query the people in your circle of trust. As I mentioned in the previous chapter, find friends, family members, or colleagues whom you believe will give you authentic feedback. Ask them to share at least five things they believe you do well. It can be very empowering to see how others perceive your strengths. Ultimately, you are in charge of what you believe you do well, those things that actually give you **strength,** but the feedback is a great point of departure on your personal strengths quest.

If you prefer a more structured approach, I recommend *Now, Discover Your Strengths*, a book by Marcus Buckingham and Donald Clifton, coupled with an online resource tool that will take you through a personalized strengths assessment.

It can be very liberating to focus on your strengths and not fixate on your weaknesses. After all, you are not broken – it's possible you simply need to unlock your passion by discovering your strengths to find the right career role.

11. WHY EVERY WOMAN NEEDS A REINVENTION TOOLBOX

It's fine to learn about great career reinventions from other women's stories. But my goal for this book is to provide you with resources and action steps so that you can create the change in your life you want to achieve.

Some career changers will recharge and reignite their careers with small scale tweaks and strength-building opportunities. Others will undergo a full scale reinvention. At the end of each chapter, I have created a *Reinvention Toolbox* packed with exercises and action steps to empower you with self-confidence and strategies to achieve your goals.

I will take you on a guided career development journey to help you get to know yourself, and to understand the importance of emotional intelligence and resiliency in the work place. I will teach you to build and steward relationships and to tap into the power of your personal resource team. You will learn from me and many fabulous women who have done it themselves, how to own your passion, take calculated risks, and live an authentic career life.

Your Guided Tour for Reinvention

You will also learn to navigate the *new normal* of this career world and become your own best advocate with the art of self-promotion. Should you decide to utilize a career coach, I will share tips and best practices to get the most from your coaching relationship. My goal is to help you make excellent choices and prioritize yourself so that you can continue to nurture your families and loved ones.

I will empower you to have the courage to put yourself first so you can thrive in a career that fits your passions and your values, interests, personality, and skills. The *Reinvention Toolbox* will help celebrate the new you – recharged, reignited, and reinvented!

Now it's time to meet, and learn from, the amazing women who have successfully transitioned and are leading gratifying new career lives.

3

TURN SURVIVE INTO THRIVE

The women in this chapter have all dealt with extreme adversity that impacted their careers. Through perseverance, positive energy, hard work, and tapping into their passions – they have turned survive into *thrive*.

12. JESSI WALTER: WHEN LIFE HANDS YOU LEMONS...MAKE CUPCAKES

A Harvard graduate with an Economics degree, Jessi Walter was the picture of success in her Vice President, six-figure position at Bear Stearns in New York City. She was young, thriving in her corporate career, and enjoying the life of an executive woman, when one day everything changed. When Bear Stearns and JP Morgan merged, Jessi was laid off. In a matter of moments the rising young executive in the New York financial district became an unemployed Ivy League grad looking for work.

From Corporate Maven to Cupcake Queen

As so many have experienced in the largest unemployment recession since the Great Depression, diving back into another job in the corporate world was not so easy. While Jessi enjoyed her Wall Street job, this new setback was really an opportunity for her to reassess her values and interests and reflect on what was really important in her life.

When life gives you lemons you make lemonade – well in this case, Jessi made cupcakes and a myriad of other delicious foods! She decided to combine her love for kids and food in a practical way. She always enjoyed cooking and although she does not have kids of her own, her family considers her the Pied Piper for kids. She enjoys spending time with her 23 first cousins and **Cupcake Kids**, which started as a hobby, but soon blossomed into a fully fledged business.

At first it began with birthday parties where she would share her culinary talents with friends who wanted to make their child's party extra special. In came Jessi, who showed the kids how to cook well-balanced and healthy foods. She taught them about math, measuring, nutrition, and following directions with a hands-on birthday celebration. The parents and the kids loved Jessi's events and soon she was a sought-after guest on the kid party circuit.

The Cupcake Kids and Katie Couric!

Tapping into her entrepreneurial spirit, Jessi developed a business plan utilizing her Harvard degree and her tenure on Wall Street. She created a company that provides experiential cooking opportunities designed to be fun and informative so that kids can learn about food and nutrition. Jessi believes that creativity plays a vital role in childhood development while helping to build self-confidence and independence.

As a Division I swimmer at Harvard, Jessi developed a competitive edge, a strong work ethic and impeccable technique. These transferable skills have served her well with **Cupcake Kids** as did the countless classes she took at the Institute of Culinary Education and the French Culinary Institute.

> "I use tons of the skills that I learned on Wall Street: everything from working with clients, to building modeling spreadsheets, to managing people. Wall Street was a great learning experience for me where I was able to delve into the business world of financing and operations. That experience has helped me immensely as I work to develop my own company. I also love connecting with people and telling them about my business.

I truly believe in what I'm doing and I know firsthand all the benefits that **Cupcake Kids** has to offer, so when I meet someone new, I find it natural to tell them all about it."

Feeding the Business

But what about the financial challenges of starting a new business? Jessi says that she is supporting herself partly from the business profit and in part from her savings as she continues to pour most of her proceeds back into the company. Recently, Jessi built a kid-friendly kitchen studio in Manhattan for young chefs (the first ever!) so she now has a home base for the business as well as the flexibility of working on location. She has other big plans in store and sees this company as an investment in her future.

Reflecting on what she knows now that she did not know when starting her business, Jessi shares that she would try to narrow her market sooner. "I've spent a lot of time trying different lines of my business. The more focused and organized a business, the better brand you build and the better your success."

While Jessi admits that time is the biggest challenge for her one-woman business, she is able to rely on advice and wisdom from her dad and grandfather – fellow entrepreneurs who have mentored her throughout this process. Jessi recently appeared on CBS Evening News with Katie Couric and it's fair to say that **Cupcake Kids** is really cookin' now!

Jessi's Advice and Action Steps:

- Take the time to develop your business plan/strategy; you can't be everything for everyone so know your market. Seek out help if you need it. This is your foundation and extremely important for new entrepreneurs.
- Do your best every day – you can always turn a negative into a positive.
- Market your new business – utilize your network. It's essential that everybody you know helps you promote your business.

- Be prepared to work harder than you ever thought possible if you start your own business – you have only yourself to rely on.
- Consider people you can hire for freelance work as needed. I hire school teachers and Chefs to help me with large parties and events. They are good with kids and appreciate the additional work on weekends and after school – it's a win-win for all.

Jessi's Resources:

Cupcake Kids! www.cupcakekids.com
Savor the Success: www.savorthesuccess.com
Ladies Who Launch: www.ladieswholaunch.com

66Knock and the door will be opened to you.99

– Book of Matthew 7:7

ℱ ℱ ℱ ℱ

13. REBECCA CARLSON: AN UNFAVORABLE DIAGNOSIS LED TO A NEW CAREER

Many people look for new careers because they are unsatisfied with their jobs, not in touch with their passion, or completely burned out. Rebecca Carlson was very happy with her career as an Art and Creative Director in the advertising world. She was playing to her strengths but feeling extremely run down, depressed, and often unable to get out of bed which was unusual for this active, athletic, and vibrant woman. Following a trip to Jamaica, her symptoms rapidly progressed to the point where she lost the feeling in her legs and found it difficult to grasp a pencil with her hand. She decided it was time to visit her doctor to see what was wrong – thinking she had pinched a nerve or something of that nature. After weeks of medical testing, countless MRIs, and two spinal taps, her doctors revealed the heartbreaking diagnosis…multiple sclerosis.

It Pays to Experiment

Her physician admitted her to the hospital and prescribed a battery of steroids, physical therapy, and medications along with the grim prediction that even with the meds, Rebecca would become wheelchair-bound, and would experience deterioration of her motor skills as well as possibly even blindness in just a matter of years as the disease progressed. Rebecca was a tenacious patient with many questions and the desire to take control of her own health. After intense research, she discovered a connection between MS and other diseases that respond well to dietary change. She figured she had nothing to lose because the best medicine available only offered a 30 percent efficacy rate, so she was determined to find a more holistic approach to healing. Against her doctor's wishes, she refused the medications and started the healing process with diet.

In the beginning she eliminated dairy, wheat/gluten, red meat, and sugar from her diet and although she still felt weak – she was functional. After viewing an episode of Diet Wars on television, Rebecca learned about the concept of raw foods. She started eating raw foods that same day because of the claims of increased energy, but much to her surprise within five days of beginning the "raw experiment" Rebecca regained her energy and her health. All of her MS symptoms had vanished. She was blown away with the results and is now a firm believer that our bodies can heal naturally if cared for properly – they were designed this way.

Be Part of the Solution

Aware that her former "normal" American diet was filled with refined carbohydrates, sugars, animal protein, caffeine, alcohol, artificial sweeteners, sodas, and fats, Rebecca was feeling incredibly energized with her new clean eating regimen with foods such as raw fruits and vegetables, nuts, seeds, sprouts, grains, healthy oils (olive and coconut) and super-foods like raw chocolate and goji berries. She was also amazed that she was able to lose 38 pounds effortlessly in the process, something she had been previously unable to do.

She found that she was telling anyone who would listen and people were amazed at her story and wanted to know more. So she committed to spreading the word and being a part of the solution rather than adding to the problem. Rebecca used her newfound energy and amazing health turnaround to cofound the business **123Raw.com** and is also the publisher of *Purely Delicious* magazine. Both are founded on the principle of taking baby steps towards a healthier body, planet, and community. Both the online store and magazine feature healthy and gourmet raw food recipes, organic and earth-friendly products for pet, home and body, fitness tips and articles about the growing raw foods movement. Nothing extreme, just regular people looking to live a little better.

It's Okay to be Afraid

Rebecca had the idea of starting a raw magazine before the online store, but was a little overwhelmed and intimidated by the idea because she wasn't sure how to get it off the ground by herself. She decided to start out with an online store first because it was something she could do from home and the hope was that it would provide the necessary funds to eventually start the magazine. Since stress exacerbates MS symptoms, she really wanted a low stress work-from-home business plan. The magazine opportunity came quite out of the blue in October of 2008. The previous publisher, Anna Tipps, was experiencing a medical emergency and contacted her to see if she was interested in taking over the publication. According to Rebecca:

> "The lesson I learned from this is, it's okay to feel fear (it's normal) but don't let it stop you in your tracks. Say yes and keep moving forward. The amazing part is that as soon as I said yes and got off the fence, people started coming out of the woodwork offering to help. Resources came to me – as they were needed."

With Rebecca determined to build a business with a conscience, **123Raw.com** contributes five percent of its profits to charities, including Habitat for Humanity and The Arbor Day Foundation, and offers one page in each magazine to a charity to bring awareness to their cause. Rebecca utilizes her many skills from the advertising arena in her new businesses; these skills include project managing, hiring freelance talent, organizing photo shoots, designing, negotiating, brainstorming, maintaining client relations, writing, meeting tight deadlines, pitching ideas, securing radio and television spots, doing press checks, etc.

Support comes from all sides and so did the opportunities. She spoke about her desire of starting a raw food magazine and *Purely Delicious* "…literally fell into her lap," according to Rebecca, which from her perspective reaffirmed that this was meant to be.

Set Practical Goals

It all sounds great, but what about the challenges of starting a new business venture? Rebecca underestimated the cost and time of starting a business: the state and local fees, the cost of filing for a trademark, web design, advertising, opening a merchant account, etc. She thought she was prepared, but in reality she knew nothing about the business end of starting a business. Though not so much in the beginning, eventually there were financial difficulties as the months dragged on and on with money going out but none coming in. She used up her savings, utilized her credit cards to get **123Raw. com** started, and then even dipped into her already dwindling 401K to pay for the first issue of *Purely Delicious*.

Her main mistake was assuming that as soon as they were open for business, customers would flock to the door. It takes time to build a brand and attract a loyal customer base. She assumed that since she had a large following on chat sites and her blog, those would automatically translate to sales. And for a large part they did, but not in the large consistent volume that was needed. With *Purely Delicious*, the problem was a little different, because she took over an existing publication and therefore was responsible for fulfilling all the subscriptions that she didn't receive payment for, so she was starting out substantially in the red. Luckily, the magazine has been extremely popular and well-received and sales have increased by 25 percent since October 2008.

Looking back, Rebecca would make some adjustments in her business launching plan.

"I think I would have searched for a business mentor to help guide me through the start-up process. I would have set more money aside and sought an open line of credit instead of relying on my personal credit. Most importantly, I would have trusted my gut instinct more. Each time I have gotten off track has been when I've ignored that 'I don't think this is right' feeling. It is a very humbling experience to realize how little you know but exhilarating to be in a constant state of learning and growth. Growth is rarely comfortable, but is necessary. I wish I would have understood this earlier."

I'm happy to report that Rebecca is thriving, feeling fit and healthy, and that both **123Raw.com** and *Purely Delicious* are gaining momentum and solvency. This little raw food experiment not only provided her a healthier life, but a new and exciting career.

Rebecca's Advice and Action Steps:

- Fear can be good if you realize it's normal. Move beyond your comfort zone and test your strengths. Have courage, acknowledge the fear, and then take a small step forward anyway.
- Give yourself practical, attainable, daily goals. Baby steps are important in the long-run journey. Try not to let yourself get overwhelmed by the enormity of the task. To climb a mountain you first have to take one step.
- Exercise random acts of kindness and pay-it-forward! Look for ways to give daily, this act also opens you up to receive.
- Consider giving back in some way with your business in your community.

Rebecca's Resources:

123 Raw: www.123Raw.com
Purely Delicious: www.PurelyDelicious.net
Savor the Success: www.savorthesuccess.com
Organic Consumers Organization: www.organicconsumers.org/

"When you are willing to try, amazing things can happen"

– Rebecca Carlson

"It takes a lot of courage to show your
dreams to someone else."

– Erma Bombeck

ℰ ℰ ℰ ℰ

14. MARY MCMANUS: A GIFT FROM THE HEART

Mary McManus, Boston Marathon finisher, inspirational speaker, published poet, entrepreneur and former award-winning social worker, turned adversity on its head after being diagnosed with postpolio syndrome in December 2006. Mary turned to writing inspirational poetry to heal her life. She never imagined the path that would unfold before her.

A Brave New World

At the age of 53, Mary was diagnosed with postpolio syndrome, a result of her original polio affliction that had begun when she was just five years old. Despite the diagnosis, she always persevered and made the best of a very difficult physical situation, getting around with a cane or a wheelchair as her condition got worse.

After 25 years as a social worker with the Department of Veterans Affairs in Boston, Massachusetts, Mary was eager to finish three more years at her job so that she could retire with full benefits. The postpolio syndrome became increasingly debilitating and there were days when Mary could literally not get out of bed. She worked with a team of occupational and physical therapists to help get her to the three-year retirement goal, but ultimately continuing to work at the VA was counter-therapeutic to the gains she was making in rehab.

Her job as a social worker at the Department of Veterans Affairs was incapacitating, both physically and emotionally, so based on the advice of her doctors Mary, with a heavy heart, left her award-winning career in May of 2007. But Mary is a deeply spiritual person and believed that divine intervention was part of her new life; she began to write as part of her catharsis and personal therapy.

Poetic Justice

Mary always loved to write and she created original poetry to commemorate and celebrate special occasions for family and friends. She recalled that the poems just flowed out of her after she left her job as a social worker and she then knew that there was a bright future ahead and a new career opportunity. Mary's husband encouraged her to create **New World Greeting Cards**, original poetry for every occasion.

For two years Mary grieved the loss of her career as a social worker. But she has a dream team of support in her family, and has recreated a new identity, as a poet, that has tapped her creative talents.

How does one make a living as a poet? This was a concern for Mary, too, and she pulled out her entire retirement account to fund **New World Greeting Cards** with the blessings of her husband and her daughter, Ruth Anne, who said, "You can't afford not to pursue this new poetry business, and you should write a book!" Mary believes that when you are on the right path and you believe in yourself, everything else will fall into place.

Poetry in Motion

Like any entrepreneur, Mary now has to promote her business and her brand. She has tapped into the social media resources including Twitter, Facebook, and LinkedIn. She subscribed to Help a Reporter Out to pitch her story. She authors a blog and has joined social communities including Polio Today, Daryn Kagan, and Just Finish.

Mary is a frequent guest on radio shows and also builds her audience through the polio survivor network. As a Boston University and Boston College alumna, Mary has also reaped the benefits of the alumni networks at both schools. She even took on a public relations intern from Boston University to help her grow the business. Mary has discovered "nontraditional" venues to share her journey, her books, and her business. She was invited to host a table at the Hyannis Race Expo because of her charitable donations and inspirational journey. She was an exhibitor and inspirational speaker at the 2010 Boston GreenFest sharing her journey and strategies for health and wellness.

Cognizant of the power of giving back, Mary writes gratis poems to promote awareness for the business. Examples include writing birthday poems for her friends on Facebook, an anniversary poem for a local restaurant, and a poem to commemorate her town's Department of Public Health and the first green building in the city.

Setting Sail

Mary's daughter was right about books being a part of her mother's new career. Mary discovered the gift of poetry in her soul. She has since written two books of poetry: *New World Greetings: Inspirational Poetry and Musings for a New World*, and a sequel, *Set Sail for a New World: Healing a Life Through The Gift of Poetry*. Both books are available via her website and at online book retail sites. True to Mary's belief that giving back is a part of any success story, she donates 20 percent of book proceeds to Hope Charitable Trust (to help children in India crippled by polio to walk again) and The Salk Institute for Biological Studies.

While the new career journey is scary at times, especially without a steady paycheck and benefits, Mary appreciates many new work values such as freedom, autonomy, the opportunity to create a balanced day, and being accountable only to herself.

> "I create how I want to measure success now. It's no longer by how many patients I saw in a day, and believe me it's taken awhile to let go of those values that were instilled and drilled into me after almost 20 years at the VA."

Still, there are challenges for Mary in grieving the loss of her social worker role identity.

> "I was at the top of my game as a social worker at the VA. I received many awards and accolades. Stepping way outside my comfort zone and doing something I had never done before with this business made me feel vulnerable, because I had a lack of knowledge and business savvy. Starting a new busi-

ness venture and new path in life after just being diagnosed with a progressive neurological disease is a challenge, but I'm up for the task!"

Words of Wisdom

Mary has learned to give herself quiet time to ask for direction and listen to her voice of intuition. When Mary left the VA, she used a 30-day journal with 3 sections for each day to write down her goals and action steps. She continually asks herself "What do I want to do if I know I can only succeed?" She uses a gratitude journal, giving thanks for what she has achieved and to focus on guidance for next steps.

An avid reader, Mary seeks poetic inspiration as well as life lessons from authors such as Lisa Nichols, Tony Robbins, Wayne Dyer, Terry Cole Whittaker, and Deborah Hill. Mary has given herself the gift of following her joy and bliss and makes time for creative outlets in her life. She uses exercise to manage stress and fear, and to forestall the progression of postpolio syndrome. She was limited in what she could do physically during the initial phase of her transition due to postpolio syndrome, so she turned inward to meditation and visualization to harness the power of her mind and her spirit.

Perhaps the greatest physical challenge Mary has accomplished was completing the 2009 Boston Marathon, one of the most difficult marathon courses in the country.

26.2 Miles

Mind over matter does not begin to describe Mary's tenacity and passion to overcome obstacles. She would not let postpolio syndrome get the best of her physically, so she decided to face the lion directly and push her body to the limit by running the Boston marathon.

Her daughter and husband joined her for this personal quest and trained and ran the event with her to lend their support and enthusiasm for her journey. Mary worked with a professional trainer and physical therapist to get her into marathon shape.

Team McManus crossed the finish line of the 113th Boston Marathon at 4:49 p.m., 7 hours and 49 minutes after taking their start at

Hopkinton, Massachusetts, along with mobility and visually impaired runners. In the ultimate gesture of giving back, *Team McManus raised over $10,000 for Spaulding Rehab Hospital – the facility which helped Mary take the first steps on her healing journey.*

Conquering Heartbreak Hill

The Boston Marathon is known for the treacherous Heartbreak Hill segment of the course that challenges the most accomplished of runners. Mary tackled Heartbreak Hill and crossed the finish line of the marathon, which is a metaphor for her life. She is a woman who overcomes obstacles.

Now that the marathon is over, Mary continues to manage her symptoms of postpolio syndrome, and her social security disability insurance is helping to resolve her financial challenges. She wishes she would have applied for social security disability benefits sooner so that she would have freed up her creative energies, rather than doing a lot of reacting out of fear about her finances.

New World Greeting Cards is going well and Mary continues to develop new ways to increase her business presence. Original poems begin at $20 for a card and $50 for a keepsake poem. Mary works with clients individually to customize keepsake poetry for one-of-a-kind gifts.

Her future goals include working with Rotary Clubs to eradicate polio and raise awareness and monies to fund research for polio and postpolio syndrome. She also looks to expand her network for inspirational talks, and book signings, and has another book project in the works with Bernie Siegel, MD, about poetry and the art of healing.

Mary has brought joy, hope, healing, and celebration to others through her gift of poetry. She has overcome monumental challenges in her life and is thriving in a new career that she never would have imagined just a few years ago. As far as an award winning career? Mary was one of six finalists for 2010 Brookline Woman of the Year and was honored at their annual award ceremony "Women Who Inspire Us". She has been chosen to be interviewed by Boston's # 1 FM radio station, Magic 106.7, for its Exceptional Women Show. Indeed it is a new world for Mary McManus and a brilliant reinvention.

Mary's Advice and Action Steps:

- Give some of your talents away and the rewards will come back tenfold.
- Check out your local Chamber of Commerce for a fabulous networking resource.
- Tune into your passion and tune out voices of negativity.
- Develop a dream team of support.

Resources:

New World Greeting Cards: www.newworldgreetings.com

Help a Reporter Out: www.helpareporter.com/

Boston Marathon news feature:
  www.youtube.com/marysunshine100

Mary's Running Inspiration: www.runnerinsight.com/2009/04/27/
  marys-boston-marathon-literally-unstoppable/

The starting line at Hopkinton: www.twitpic.com/3dac7

"I missed 100 percent of the shots I never took."

– Michael Jordan

15. CAROLE BRODY FLEET: A WIDOW LEARNS TO HEAL IN HIGH HEELS

At the young age of 40, Carole Brody Fleet had a thriving career in the cosmetics industry. She built a new house from her Mary Kay Cosmetics earnings; she was a national winner of top sales awards and numerous accolades. But none of her success could soothe the deep pain she experienced when her husband died after a two-year battle with Lou Gehrig's disease. A young widow, with a then 11-year-old-daughter, Carole had days when she literally could not get out of bed.

Loss is ageless, but the issues young widows deal with are unique. Five years after her husband's death, Carole had begun to recover financially, though massive medical bills had depleted her bank account, even with a steady income. After the long journey of emotional healing she was ready to share her widow's wisdom with others who had experienced a loss. She wanted to utilize her experiences to educate women who needed a resource, and thus her writing career began. It has since become her passion and life mission to bring the message of hope, promise, and abundance to those who have been touched by the pain and challenge of widowhood, regardless of age.

The Things People Don't Tell You

Carole scoured the available grief and bereavement books to help her through the difficult times after her husband's death. What frustrated her most was the lack of information about what to do next, after the grief. She needed help getting her benefits from the government, battling with insurance companies, and dealing with the nitty-gritty details of widowhood that nobody was willing to discuss out loud.

She needed help with practical and financial transitioning back into the world of the living. Carole was a young and attractive woman but she struggled with the widow stigma and often felt guilty if she put on makeup or her signature high heels. And what about dating again? Could she ever consider romance again or was she doomed to be a lifelong widow wearing black?

The Black Widow

Carole remembers a lucid moment at her husband's funeral when she realized she was technically a widow but did not want to succumb to the stereotypical image of a widow – she wore stilettos after all!

Current research tells us that 40 percent of single mothers in the U.S. are widows. Carole was more determined than ever to build a support network for other women; she began a series of public speaking engagements and became known as the "inspiration lady." Appreciative widows came out of the woodwork to begin their healing journey with Carole and her audience grew from local presentations to national appearances like ABC's *Good Morning America* and a feature article in *Women's World* magazine.

In order to focus her new calling and tap into her longtime joy of writing, Carole penned the book *Widows Wear Stilettos: A Practical and Emotional Guide for the Young Widow*. She also authored and served as executive producer for her CD, *Widows Wear Stilettos: What Now?* Carole's goal is to effect positive change and help women deal with the realities of widowhood with answers to the tough questions nobody else was willing to address.

Widow on a Mission

In addition to her many national multimedia appearances on radio, TV, and as a motivational speaker, Carole's Widows Wear Stiletto's website is widely recognized as a leading resource in bereavement recovery. She receives between 800 and 1000 new messages from widows each week and takes pride in reading each one.

The plight of the young widow is unique and Carole's niche market approach deals with issues such as:

- Taking ownership of your personal healing journey.
- Coping with the comments, opinions, and insights that you may encounter from others.
- Fashion, beauty, diet and exercise tips including quick and easy recipes.
- Advice on how and when to re-enter the world of dating and what to do once you get there.
- Financial and practical transitioning with how-to suggestions, check lists, and guidelines.
- Helping children of all ages adapt and transition after the loss of a parent.

In addition, Carole also provides personal coaching to help widows move forward in their healing. Fully aware that some clients need the care of medical or psychiatric professionals, Carole's coaching intent is to serve as a complementary resource, as a widow who has walked in those shoes.

You'll Never Walk Alone

The journey of authoring books has indeed been a challenge as the publishing industry is inundated with new authors. For every twenty-five million writers, only five percent get publishing contracts. But Carole was determined to help others and developed a thick skin; with her resilience and tenacity she landed a contract with New Horizon Press. Her newest publication, *Widows Wear Stilettos: The Answer Book – The Ultimate Question, Answer and Reference Guide for Widows*, is forthcoming.

The most important message Carole provides is that widows have resources and a large network of fellow widows for support and encouragement. The empowerment of widows is what drives Carole on a daily basis, and above all, the message is that these women are not alone.

Life Support for Widows

Widowhood is a frightening prospect for any woman, but the reality of becoming a widow in your forties, thirties or twenties can be terrifying. Not only must one face normal grief, but also the additional painful issues that arise with the death of a young person. Because of catastrophic events such as the World Trade Center tragedy and the Gulf and Iraqi Wars, the demographic of young widows has grown suddenly and dramatically.

Carole's books, website, and motivational speeches have proven to be a form of life support for many young widows. She has been featured in many magazines, newspapers and websites, including: *Psychology Today, The Houston Chronicle, More, Cosmopolitan, Military Officer, Philadelphia Daily News* and *Orange County Register.* She was a featured contributor in the *Hartford Courant* and *Boston Metro News* and continues to write articles in national publications.

Today Carole resides in Lake Forest, California, with her daughter, three cats and over 100 pairs of shoes. Yes, this widow has begun a new life and is dedicated to helping others who have experienced a devastating loss do the same.

Carole's Advice and Action Steps:

- Not everyone is going to love what you do or the choices you make – let it roll.
- Develop a thick skin and believe in yourself.
- The motivation for me to do good things for others is stronger than seeking a job that just pays the bills.

Resources:

Widows Wear Stilettos www.widowswearstilettos.com

"Focusing on '*Why me?*' for too long does nothing to change your situation or further healing. Choosing instead to focus on '*What now?*'…will!"

– Carole Brody Fleet

ᔕ ᔕ ᔕ ᔕ

16. TAKE A STEP FORWARD

The women in this chapter changed careers because life dealt them very difficult situations to overcome. Jessi Walter's Wall Street career was a casualty of the recession. Rebecca Carlson and Mary McManus overcame debilitating diseases that left them physically unable to do their former jobs. Carole Brody Fleet became a widow at a young age and her world turned upside down. But each of these women found a new beginning and they are thriving in different careers.

What inspires me most about these women is their ability to face the unknown, as well as their fears. Many people resist career change because they are afraid to take a leap into the unknown. The truth is that even without a challenging career wake-up call like each of these four women experienced, life is all about navigating the unknown.

Facing The Unknown

If you think you have carved out a career plan for your life that is set in stone – think again. There will always be constant changes beyond your control and that's okay. Life is change and if you are able to tap into your adaptability and resilience you will always land on your feet.

Likewise, if you are in a career you dislike, you have the power to change that. I encourage you to loosen the mental grip you have on your life that is preventing you from considering the change that will empower you to reinvent yourself and your career. If you find the courage to consider change, you will muster the energy to transform your career and your life. By being proactive, you can find a new career that brings you joy, or you can let life impose change on you. Reading this book is a positive step towards being proactive. Cheers to you!

REINVENTION TOOLBOX

Know Thy Self; Showcase Your Resilience; Utilize Soft Skills

After reading about the *survive-to-thrive* women in this chapter, I hope you are inspired by how they are flourishing after dealing with incredibly difficult situations that impacted their lives and careers. These four action steps will help you thrive as you begin to develop the new and reinvented you.

Action Step #1: Take the time for self-reflection to discover what is really important to you. Think about your values, interests, personality, and skills and connect these dots to find career opportunities that match the real you. Consider your career passions. What occupation(s) would you pursue if you had no obstacles in your way? Get quiet with yourself and reflect – a true self-assessment takes time and focus.

Action Step #2: Write it down! Use this book as a career journal to write down detailed thoughts about your VIPS, hopes, dreams, and goals. Store a pocket-sized notebook in your purse so that you have it with you on the go and can jot down impromptu thoughts and inspirations. Putting your wishes on paper helps you articulate things more clearly and gives you accountability for achieving your goals.

Take a close look at the next 90 days and write down what you want to accomplish. You can always change your mind and adjust your game plan, but dig deep to think about what you really want. Split your 90-day goal into smaller, attainable actions and chop it into manageable baby steps. Research tells us that you are 90 times more likely to accomplish a goal when it is written down. What are you waiting for? Grab a pen and write down your goals!

Action Step #3: Showcase your resiliency! Now more than ever employers want to see that you can bounce back and recover quickly from adversity. Resilience is a key competency that employers value because it transfers well into the workplace. One constant in every career field is change. If you can show an employer that you can deal with change you can be seen as a valuable commodity to that organization. Attitude is just as important as your skill set in a competitive marketplace.

If you were downsized out of your last job, pick yourself up and get back on that proverbial career horse. Showcase this adaptive skill to illustrate that you are scrappy, flexible, and able to recover from a setback with a positive attitude and a game plan. There is no room in this job market for a negative attitude, and badmouthing your former employer is the kiss of death. Put your game face on and forge ahead with confidence.

I have seen negative attitudes get the best of amazing job candidates because the applicants are still grieving the loss of a former position and have not let go emotionally. Take the time you need to vent, rant, and rave in the privacy of your own home – this is therapeutic and essential to establish a new and positive mindset. But when you are ready (sooner is better than later!) focus and concentrate on your goals. Put your best professional foot forward and show the job world that you are ready for a new opportunity.

Action Step #4: Utilize Your Soft Skills. Quite often people brush off the soft skills as the touchy feely people skills that serious professionals don't need. Nothing could be farther from the truth! The soft skills include abilities and traits such as self-awareness, initiative, time management, empathy, political astuteness, integrity, and many more.

Tap into your emotional intelligence and consider seriously how you perform in these four areas:

- **Self-awareness** – The ability to recognize your own emotions and how they affect your thoughts and behavior, know your strengths and weaknesses, and exhibit self-confidence.

- **Self-management** – The ability to control impulsive feelings and behaviors, manage your emotions in healthy ways, take initiative, follow through on commitments, and adapt to changing circumstances.

- **Social awareness** – The ability to understand the emotions, needs, and concerns of other people, pick up on emotional cues, feel comfortable socially, and recognize the power dynamics in a group or organization.

- **Relationship management** – The ability to develop and maintain good relationships, communicate clearly, inspire and influence others, work well on a team, and manage conflict.

Some people enjoy a self-directed assessment, and others work better utilizing a coach who can lead them through the self-discovery process. I am here as a resource for you if you prefer a customized plan. You can email me through my website www.carolinedowdhiggins.com.

4

BECOME A MEMBER OF THE CREATIVITY CLUB

The Creativity Club women each tapped into her experience, resourcefulness, and innovation to reinvent her career.

17. STACEY KANNENBERG: MOM-ON-A-MISSION BUILDS PUBLISHING EMPIRE

After 14 years in corporate America, Stacey made the decision, while she was pregnant with her first child, to stay home and raise her family. It was a life-changing move. This suburban Wisconsin mom was not a teacher by training, but she went on to create kindergarten and first grade books now used in schools across the nation. Now a successful author, publisher, motivator, consultant, and mom, Stacey is nationally renowned as an education expert.

From Strollers to First Grade

So how did this all begin? When Stacey's first daughter was a toddler, Stacy walked the neighborhood with other moms and like many American women, she tuned into Oprah daily for entertainment and inspiration. Like a good mom, Stacey was eager to prepare her young daughter for the new world of Kindergarten and tried to find resources they could use together to help with this transition to formal education. Alas, there were none.

A lot had changed since Stacey could still remember first grade, let alone kindergarten. There was new terminology and a different language that seemed foreign to this corporate mogul turned full-time mom. Partly to help other families of the same generation understand how to help their kids and to better prepare their little ones for this new school adventure, Stacey developed *Let's Get Ready for Kindergarten*, a resource that was a big hit with the children, parents, and the teachers.

The Power of the Mommy Brigade

What made these books unique was not only the content that empowered parents to bridge the proverbial generation gap with the new school language – these books were designed with durable dry erase material for every page. Ever read a book to a sticky-fingered youngster? These books were ingeniously designed to be kid friendly and mess proof.

The prototype passed muster in the neighborhood and the kids were the toughest critics helping to design the many versions before publication. But how does a first-time author publish a book? Here comes the Oprah connection! Stacey recalls the *Millionaire Mom* episode on Oprah that motivated her to make this book project a reality. She picked up additional tips from another Oprah show on self-publishing and was inspired by yet another show about Africa where youngsters asked for books to read instead of dolls to play with. Talk about tugging at your heart strings!

Stacey was a mom on a mission with a passion to get her book published and that is what she did. Along the way, she had the unconditional support of her husband and kids, who she calls her "saving grace" during this publishing journey; it was a journey which included times of frustration and challenge. Stacey is committed to paying-it-forward by helping other moms realize their entrepreneurial dreams.

How did she get published? Oprah's show on self-publishing was the first time Stacey had seriously thought about self-publishing her book. She researched self-publishing online and found many people who raved about Dan Poynter.

"To me he is the Oprah of Self-Publishing. I read Dan Poynter's *The Self-Publishing Manual* and followed the steps in his book. I found a local printer who introduced me to Two Bit Productions and they were willing to take a chance on me to do my illustrations and website. They believed in what I was trying to do and were willing to work with me to bring it to life. They believed so much in the mission that they were willing to tear up their bill if it was a flop. Having their faith gave me the courage to soar! Thinking back, they took a great risk and I would never be where I am today without them and many other people, many of whom I did NOT really know all that well, who believed in what I was trying to do and stepped up to the plate to offer words of encouragement or forged connections to get me to the next step."

Amazed by the number of people who believed in her to the point that they became brand evangelists sharing the news about her books to teachers and schools, Stacey truly believes in the power of networking. She decided to do a small press run of 3,000 books and did not order an ISBN number (this number needs to be coded on the back of the book in order for it to be sold by major distributors, such as Barnes & Noble and Amazon). Stacey thought she would have the rest of her life to sell those 3,000 copies and literally drove around from school to school and bookstore to bookstore selling books out of her car. The book was featured in the local newspaper and then TMJ4 Milwaukee Television did a story which had Paula Jones from Barnes & Noble calling and asking to carry her books. Paula helped Stacey get the all-important ISBN number and get the books into the National Barnes & Noble retailer and set up numerous book-signing opportunities.

Creating Life on Her Terms

Was it easy? No! Stacey had to jump over her fair share of hurdles and had many a dark day, but so many people believed in what she was trying to do that she took baby steps which advanced her project to a profitable business. According to Stacey, "I bootstrapped and self-funded my business from day one!"

"I love an Oprah quote that really resonated with me from one of her shows: 'Obstacles are really just opportunities in disguise.' It is so true. Every obstacle along the way has turned out to be a blessing. I had the amazing support of my family, who I empowered to join the process. I mean, who better to help me write 'Let's get Ready for Second Grade' than Megan, who just finished second grade and Heidi, who just finished fourth! My husband gave me a clear crystal clock in 2004 for the first Christmas celebrating **Cedar Valley Publishing**. He had the logo engraved along with a phrase he coined that has since become my mantra: *The Dream is Clear to Believe is the Reward*. I can't tell you how many times a day I look at that clock and it makes me smile and it keeps me going because the dream is crystal clear for me. This concept has become bigger than my products – it has morphed into a movement to empower parents, kids and teachers to work together to change education starting at the core – preschool and kindergarten!"

Stacey is fiercely passionate about helping others learn from her experiences. "One of my challenges was in trying to build my own Google footprint for my titles and my company. It took a long while before I realized that the one thing that ties us all together is my name – and I hadn't even thought about branding that. If I was to do it all over I would have named my book 'Kindergarten'. Had I done that I would have been using my key search word as my title without any other words to get in the way of people finding my kindergarten book."

With a powerful personal network that started with the playgroup mommies, Stacey is the Founder and CEO of two publishing companies: **Cedar Valley Publishing** and **Stacey Kannenberg Unlimited**. By the way, Cedar Valley was the street Stacey used to walk along with her young daughter in a stroller, so how fitting that she chose this name for her first business.

The Spanish/English edition of *Let's Get Ready for Kindergarten! ¡A Prepararse Para Kindergarten!* was released in February of 2009 and has already sold 3,000 copies. Overall, Stacey has all sold over 60,000 copies of her three titles.

This entrepreneurial mom made her mark by designing a much needed resource for parents and kids. Using her transferable skills from the corporate arena and honoring her values as a mom who wants to raise her own children, Stacey made this career move work based on her terms.

Stacey's Advice and Action Steps:

- If you are starting a business, find a niche market. No one ever thought of a national Kindergarten text book – and it took off!
- Consider a platform based on need. What is the need of your client base – do your research.
- Tap into your personal network. The Mommy and Daddy Brigade is a powerful group; learn from each other.
- Seek out mentors and supporters who share your values and mission.
- Believe that one person can make a difference!

Resources:

Cedar Valley Publishing: www.cedarvalleypublishing.com
Savor the Success: www.savorthesuccess.com
$10,000 a month for the best idea: www.ideablob.com/
Publicity opportunities at: www.parapublishing.com

“The dream is clear to believe is the reward.”

– Mike Kannenberg

18. Carla Falcone and Romy Taormina: Turning Morning Sickness Into a Business Enterprise

Carla Falcone and Romy Taormina met and became fast friends at an award-winning advertising agency on California's Central Coast many years ago. Carla has an extensive background in public relations and advertizing and earned degrees in journalism and industrial arts. Romy has an in-depth knowledge of marketing and earned a business degree.

These women have extensive experience strategizing, creating, and executing multimedia campaigns for a myriad of clients in a variety of industries. But their entrepreneurial spirit blossomed after both women experienced ongoing morning sickness during their respective pregnancies. In fact, at Carla's baby shower the two were commiserating about the drab gray acupressure wrist bands that were helping Carla keep her morning sickness at bay. She was no longer nauseous but the dull wristbands did nothing to enhance her adorable maternity outfit!

With 20+ years of collective marketing experience, Romy and Carla hit the mother-load of ideas and conceived the plan for a more fashionable and functional acupressure wrist band. Two years later **Psi Bands** (pronounced "sigh") was born.

Ancient Wisdom Meets FDA Standards

Psi Bands use acupressure, an ancient healing art supported by scientific studies, to relieve nausea when placed at the Nei-kuan acupressure points on the wrists. These drug-free wrist bands help relieve nausea in a natural way. **Psi Bands** have been used successfully to help those suffering from motion sickness, post surgical anesthesia nausea, and chemotherapy-induced nausea, in addition to those suffering from morning sickness. Wrist acupressure is widely used for the relief of nausea because it is noninvasive, easy to self-administer, and affordable. These FDA-cleared bands are now available in major retail stores nationwide and internationally.

Romy and Carla are on a mission to provide high quality, fashionable, comfortable, and affordable products that make a positive difference in the lives of people suffering from nausea. If that weren't impressive enough, **Psi Bands** donates a percentage of its profits to *Fertile Hope*, a LIVE**STRONG** initiative dedicated to providing reproductive information, support, and hope to cancer patients and survivors whose medical treatments present the risk of infertility.

Back of a Napkin Idea to Sustainable Business

These women have a wealth of marketing and advertising experience between them but how did they actually get this product off the ground? Romy told me that the initial product sketches were drafted on the back of a napkin! Friend and colleague Peter Schouten joined the women in the business, and his expertise in product design and development was the perfect complement to the PR and marketing expertise of Carla and Romy.

Romy and Carla knew from the get-go that they were onto something when they conceived the idea for **Psi Bands**. After extensive research, the two women decided that they had a solid business model and quit their day jobs. They admit it was a scary leap of faith, but a necessity to make it a sustainable business. Since they love what they do and love that they are helping people in the process, Romy and Carla know they made the right choice.

Work/family balance is their largest challenge, but they enjoy their work and would not have it any other way. Romy reported: "We try to stay 'in' the moment – whether it is with our children or working on the business." With 20/20 hindsight, the women know now that some of their hiring choices would have been different if they had to do it over again. They would start with a focus on ensuring that their team members share the company's goals and vision.

Future goals for **Psi Bands** include continuing to build brand awareness, landing some additional large retailers nationally, and growing the international expansion. At the end of the day, Romy and Carla both believe you must love what you do. These mothers of invention are thriving!

Romy and Carla's Advice and Action Steps:

- Be sure your partners and employees/consultants have the same goal and vision for the company as you do.
- Seek out the advice and expertise of others when you don't have the experience to make an informed decision.
- Join womens entrepreneur groups to network, find inspiration, and share ideas.
- Follow your dreams, do what you love, and believe in yourself!
- Listen to your gut, do your research, and believe in your product/service 100 percent. Your passion will need to carry you through the inevitable business challenges that you will face.

Resources:

Psi Bands: www.psibands.com
Make Mine a Million $ Business: www.makemineamillion.org
National Association of Women's Business Owners (NAWBO):
 www.nawbo.org
Savor the Success: www.savorthesuccess.com
The Mom Entrepreneur Support Group: www.themomentrepreneur.com
Ladies Who Launch: www.ladieswholaunch.com

❝There will be bumps. Savor the journey.❞

– Carla Falcone and Romy Taormina

19. HEIDI ROIZEN: GET INTO YOUR SKINNY JEANS

Heidi Roizen is a household name for many, recognized for success as an entrepreneur, a corporate executive, a corporate director, and venture capitalist. She has also held positions of leadership within a number of industry organizations, and is a sought-after spokesperson for the technology industry and entrepreneurial community. So why did an incredibly successful career woman need a new project to add to her already full career plate?

> "As they say, necessity is the mother of invention, and I can say for certain that *SkinnySongs* exists because I really, really needed it. In May of 2007, I got on the scale, and the numbers were a disaster – at 190, not only was I at an all-time high, but for the first time I weighed more than my husband, and he's not a small guy.

> Cursing myself, I vowed that I would change, this time for real. My 50th birthday loomed only months away, and I promised myself that I would fit into my skinny jeans again by then – but with close to forty pounds between them and me, I had some serious work to do."

The Power of Inspiration

And so Heidi was on a mission to lose weight and get into shape, but she realized that if she was going to resist her old temptations and get mentally prepared for her lifestyle shift, she would need some inspiration. Since music had always been a powerful force in her life, she looked for songs that would inspire her to stick to the new healthy living plan and get her back into her skinny jeans; but alas – there was nothing that fit the bill. Ever the entrepreneur, Heidi set out to create a CD filled with music to inspire and empower her, and others, to get through this daunting and long-term personal challenge of shedding the weight and staying healthy, for life.

> " I started penning lyrics that would inspire me to stick to my plan – songs about my relationship with food and my need to become 'the boss' of that relationship, a love song to my skinny jeans, a fantasy song about fitting into designer clothes, a song reminding me to get up and move."

Heidi is a woman of many talents but a musician she is not, so after writing the lyrics for *Skinny Songs* she set out to enlist some of the best producers and talented emerging artists in the music business and enticed them to work on her new project. Starting with the expertise of Dave Malloy and George Daly as producers, the team grew to include Tania Hancheroff, Kaleo Sallas, Larkin Gayl, Rachelle Byrne, and Susan Ashton who provided vocals for the project. Lori Sutherland was onboard as Consulting Producer and ensured that the project became a monster hit.

Heidi reports that during the actual CD recording and production process the artistic team lost weight and became determined to live healthier lives. The inspiration and results began even before the recording was available to the general public.

> "Of course, it wasn't just the music – I also made a personal commitment to take charge of my life, to stop coming up with excuses. As a lifelong yo-yo dieter, I knew that what I needed was a set of permanent lifestyle changes that I could live with, on both the 'input' and the 'output' side of the equation. I'm pleased to report that I am 40+ pounds lighter and went from a size 14 to a size 8. And I still listen to the music EVERY DAY, especially in my car when I am heading to an event where I know I'll be tempted."

Turning a Personal Quest into a Profitable Venture

SkinnySongs served a personal mission in Heidi's life but as a savvy businesswoman, she also knew it had money-making potential. As with any new project she took on, *SkinnySongs* forced her to dive in, do the research, and run the numbers to determine if this project was viable and worth her investment. Heidi used her own money to finance the project and was committed to doing it very well; she hired the best in the music industry to realize her goal. She took an entire year off to work on this labor of love but admits that she does not want *SkinnySongs* to be the platform of her main career.

As a small business, *SkinnySongs* runs on its own today with CD and merchandise sales bringing in profits. Heidi and *SkinnySongs* have been featured widely, including appearances on *The Martha Stewart Show*, *CBS Early Morning*, *Oprah & Friends Radio* and *CNN*. *SkinnySongs* is available on Amazon and iTunes. But Heidi's physical reinvention also led her to consider some additional lifestyle changes. After many years in the heart of the corporate world, Heidi realized that at 51 she had a new set of values. She no longer defined success by a high-powered CEO career and wanted more variety and control over the time in her life.

SkinnySongs served as a catalyst for change and reinvention in Heidi's career and personal life. Not only did she shed the pounds and embrace a healthy lifestyle, she considered what was most important in her life and discovered that she wanted intellectual stimulation in her work, but also the time to spend with her family and to maintain her new healthy habits.

Reinventing Yourself Personally and Professionally

She is now embracing a new career in public governance and took this new role very seriously by attending Director's College to learn the essentials of serving on Boards of companies. Heidi wants to serve companies that are good investments and that pay Board members with equities, but she vows she must have a passion for their product. Currently, she serves on the Board of Directors for TiVo Inc. and Yellow Pages Group.

With these new opportunities in public governance, Heidi has more control over her time and can focus on her husband and teenage girls and still get in a good workout daily while pursuing a meaningful career. While *SkinnySongs* empowered Heidi with the confidence to lead a healthy life, Heidi also inspired many others to do the same. She feels proud that *SkinnySongs* is helping others and also allowed her to "…focus, deliver, and get out of my old head space and define a new head space and goals."

Careers change over time and it's empowering to know that we can all be more in control of our career destiny. We all have unique goals and aspirations for career and life so take the time to consider yours. Have you worn your skinny jeans lately?

Heidi's Advice and Action Steps:

- Spend some time getting to know yourself – what you like, what you don't like, strengths and interests. Don't play to your weaknesses – focus on your strengths!
- Get some distance between yourself and what you did before. Wind down to zero, be quiet and listen to your SELF. What do you want? So many of us rarely consider this.
- A woman's career is like a marathon run in segments. What is your 5-year, 10-year, 15-year plan? Chances are you will be working a long time so give yourself the liberty of changing your career course as you wish.
- To craft a career change, think about combining your skills and strengths with a current need in the economy or your community – whatever niche you want to fill.

Resources:

SkinnySongs: www.skinnysongs.com
Heidi's Personal Website: www.heidiroizen.com

❝That which does not kill us makes us stronger.**❞**

– Friedrich Nietzsche

20. GRACE CHON: FROM THE AD AGENCY TO PUPPY LOVE

A self-proclaimed *crazy dog lady*, Grace Chon grew up wanting to be a veterinarian. She majored in biology as an undergraduate and volunteered in animal hospitals to really test-drive the profession before committing to vet school. Her Korean immigrant parents were auguring for medical school, so that Grace could be a physician for humans instead of animals, but in the end Grace surprised everybody and opted for art school where she earned a Masters of Fine Arts.

Little Doggie Lips

She had a very successful career in a huge advertising agency in Los Angeles working on campaigns for national brands including Panda Express, Saturn cars, eBay Motors, Shutterfly and The San Francisco Giants, to name just a few. As an Art Director, she was responsible for full-scale guerilla marketing from websites to TV commercials and everything between. The work was exciting and fast paced but after many years it left her stressed out, unbalanced, and unhealthy.

As a way to relieve her stress, Grace began to take photos of homeless dogs at the local animal shelters in order to help them find loving homes. As an Art Director, she had developed a wonderful eye and worked with photographers regularly so she knew the craft even though she was not formally trained in the medium.

The hobby morphed into a sideline business and Grace began working early mornings, late nights, and weekends on her photography in addition to her ad agency job. She was clocking over 70 hours per week and received a significant raise at the agency after launching a popular national television campaign. But after nine months of the cottage industry business and the grind of the day job, Grace quit the ad agency to focus on her photography full-time. This woman, in love with organic gardening, old books, and little doggie lips recognized her calling and took the leap.

Do You Zig or Zag?

Grace's background in advertising gave her the perfect set of transferable skills to launch her new business and make it a successful full-time venture. She designed her own website, developed her brand, and marketed the business in order to attract clients. Grace uses social media resources to spread the word about her business including a blog (www.shinepetphotos.com/blog/) that has become very popular with clients.

While Grace capitalized on her self-reliance, she also knows the importance of distinguishing herself and her work. Since the time Grace launched **ShinePetPhotos**, over 70 new pet photographers have popped up in the Los Angeles area alone. She continues to be strategic and tap into her business sense to differentiate herself and separate her business from the pack.

At the ad agency she learned how to serve clients well and to solve problems. Advertising is not just marketing a product or a service, it involves solving real life problems and this has helped tremendously in her new business. Grace knew it wasn't enough to just identify her passion for animals in the form of photography – she had to monetize it in order to make a livelihood out of this new venture.

A Clear Picture of Success

When I asked Grace to distill her personal brand down to a few words she responded with *modern pet photography*. Her images are beautifully real and capture the relationship of the animal and their human families as well as the unique personality of each furry friend. She aims to capture the pets in their natural environment, with gorgeous natural light, doing their favorite things.

The adage that time is money is even more applicable according to Grace, who now works from home. She goes on location for her photography shoots, but her days are filled with hard work managing and building the business. She does find time for gardening and cooking, which was not always possible when she worked at the ad agency.

Grace feels more balanced, healthier, and has a sense of calm in her new work that everyone around her has recognized. Working with dogs and cats as your subjects takes a lot of patience. Although Grace considers herself impatient with most things in life, she has developed a sense of serenity and peace with the animals which makes for a good photo shoot.

The accolades are piling up and Grace has become widely recognized in a short period of time. She is the official photographer of *The World's Ugliest Dog Contest*, has cover photos showcased in *The Bark Magazine* and her shots were in a feature story about Perez Hilton's dog, Teddy. Grace was also named LA's best pet photographer two years in a row by *Tails Magazine*.

Grace's grit and determination have helped her transfer the ad agency skills into her own business. She is committed to doing everything she can with character and integrity and has built her business on those values. She finally feels as if she is doing what is right for her and has a sense of contentment about the new career that she is designing.

Coming Full Circle

As a little girl, Grace knew she was passionate about animals. Little did she know then that many years later she would develop a business to celebrate her furry friends and capture their essence with photographs.

Grace's friends and colleagues thought she was crazy to quit a lucrative job in the midst of a recession but she kept her eye on the prize and never looked back. In two years, her business has grown significantly. She operated in the black her very first year and nearly tripled her intake during the second year. Working full-time while growing the business was one of the most challenging things Grace has ever done, but she earned her dream career with sweat equity, business savvy, and the wisdom to know the importance of distinguishing herself from the competition.

And needless to say, she has the most lovable furry clients to work with on a daily basis, so life is grand.

Grace's Advice and Action Steps:

- Identify your passion – then monetize it!
- Be strategic and learn how to differentiate your personal brand to separate yourself from the competition. Identify your niche market.
- Know that if you start a new business you will have to work extremely hard and manage your time wisely. It's all up to you.
- Learn how to connect your transferable skills and experiences with a new opportunity.
- Develop a plan.

Resources:

Shine Pet Photos: www.shinepetphotos.com
Blog: www.shinepetphotos.com/blog

> "If you are more excited to leave your job
> on Friday than you are to come in to work
> on Monday, something is wrong."

– Donny Deutsch

ლ ლ ლ ლ

21. TAKE A STEP FORWARD

The women in this chapter tapped into their creativity to launch new career opportunities. Stacey Kannenberg, Carla Falcone, Romy Taormina, Heidi Roizen and Grace Chon all had safe and practical careers they could have stayed with, or gone back to, but they chose to pursue new ventures that spoke to their passions.

As entrepreneurs, these women filled a need with their products and found their unique niche market. They also tapped into their networks and built resource teams that could help them achieve their new goals.

Don't Wait Until You Need a Network to Build One

Building professional relationships is not something you do only when you need a job or promotion. It's not something you can force, buy, or borrow days before you need it. Developing meaningful relationships should be a regular part of your life as a success-oriented individual. Just like friendships, the most authentic and meaningful professional relationships evolve naturally over time.

Stacey Kannenberg tapped into the mommy network, which is a powerful resource of talented women who are currently focusing on raising their children. Don't overlook the obvious; count all the people around you as members of your prospective network from the playground to the board room. One of the best ways to grow your network is through personal referrals from your friends and family.

Believe in Yourself

These women launched risky new businesses and went against the pack by **not** doing the safe, reasonable, and secure thing. They all had naysayers discouraging them from moving forward with their plans, but they were able to filter out the negatives and focus on the positives because they had the strength and conviction to believe in themselves.

The group mentality is often fear based but these women broke through the pack and showcased their innovation and individuality. How do you want to be seen in the world? As one who follows the crowd or, as a cutting-edge thinker and leader? By honoring yourself and building a support system of people who share your vision, you can create and thrive in the new career you want, whether it is an entrepreneurial venture or a new profession.

REINVENTION TOOLBOX

Build Relationships – Not Networks; Tap into Your Resource Team

I believe that the six degrees of separation theory is being whittled down since not a day goes by that I don't make a valuable connection with a new person based on a referral from someone I already know. The women in this chapter also utilized their respective networks to move forward with their new career goals.

Having successfully reinvented my career, I am confident that I can achieve my dreams; but I have also realized that I can't do it all alone. My personal Board of Directors and mentor team has provided a valuable opportunity for me to cultivate and nurture quality relationships. I don't like to think in terms of increasing my network; instead, I build my community!

Good things happen through other good people, so I encourage you to build quality relationships and think about how you can help others in addition to getting what you need from your personal posse.

In the career world, 80 percent of jobs are unadvertised and these positions are landed through the power of networking. Whether you are seeking a new position, launching an entrepreneurial venture, or marketing your wares or services in an existing business, building and stewarding professional relationships will help you on your way. Here are some best practices to lead you to success:

1. **Ask yourself what your goals are** in developing networking relationships so that you can seek out individuals who will help you gather relevant information.
2. **Know your personal brand.** Have a clear understanding of what you do well and what makes you special or different from others doing the same thing. In order to get referrals, you must be able to articulate what your brand or *special sauce* is to others.
3. **Know what you want.** Be able to articulate what you are seeking and how others may help you – and how you can reciprocate.
4. **Stay Positive.** Be prepared to speak with anyone who will listen; don't be afraid of rejection. Be friendly and put yourself out there.
5. **Search out a common denominator.** Figure out the common interests you share with those with whom you speak. Build the conversation around that topic to get the ball rolling and ease nerves.
6. **Take risks** and reach out to some *wish list* contacts or join a professional group that could lead to something significant.
7. **Become known as a powerful resource for others.** When you are known as a strong resource, people will

turn to you for suggestions, ideas, and referrals. This keeps you visible to them and gives you a chance to give back.

8. **Make yourself useful.** Reach out to others in a capacity where you can actually do something good and show off your skills at the same time. Join a board of a worthy organization; offer to take notes at a conference where people in your desired career sector will be, and look for opportunities to solve problems.

8. **Be gracious and always thank the people** (in writing) who have been helpful. Stewarding relationships in your network is essential for your professional reputation and it's most appreciated.

When I launched my blog, career development experts came out of the woodwork to check out the site. It was a wonderful way for me to connect with new colleagues in the field and exchange valuable resources. Paul Marrangoni authors a great website called *The Practical Mentor* and he shared these words on the power of mentorship.

"Mentors are the beacons of experience whose advice and guidance can make all the difference between success and opportunities lost. Although we are each individuals facing unique situations and challenges, common threads of human nature run through all of us. So, while our perception of circumstances and challenges are unique, there is a universal quality to knowledge and experience. Each of us must make our own choices and decisions, but we do not have to do it alone. Just imagine where we would be if we each of us had to invent our own conveniences? How long do you think it would take you to decide to teach yourself just to make fire? It took all humanity thousands of years. Why not take advantage of the wealth of knowledge that mentors have to offer? You may be pleasantly surprised at the results." *The Practical Mentor* www.practicalmentor.com

5

LEARN A LESSON FROM THE RECOVERING LAWYERS

I work with many lawyers in my capacity as a Director of Career and Professional Development at the Indiana University Maurer School of Law. While some attorneys thrive in their legal careers throughout their professional lives, others utilize their transferable skills to find new careers that play to their strengths and speak to their passions. The women in this chapter have found a new life after the law and are relishing their new beginnings.

22. ELLEN COVNER: FROM LAW TO LANDSCAPING

Early in her career, Ellen Covner, like many other professional women, noticed that working with men could be a very mixed experience. She also learned that group and workplace dynamics often had a style and language all their own that did not promote cooperation, creativity, and "drive." She came to realize that as important as it was to be self-supporting and have a good income, money was not a sufficient motivator to stay in a "good job." After 20+ years practicing health law in major hospitals and law firms, she was ready for new challenges. She wanted a change that would renew her creativity and joy in her work. The call of the outdoors beckoned and enticed her to focus on promoting environments that nourish people and their properties.

A Circuitous Route to Career Bliss

Moving from a secure and high powered career in law to the world of an entrepreneur was no easy task. Ellen discussed the transition with friends, family, and her husband, all of whom supported her in this daring new career move. She phased into landscaping, keeping her hand in the legal world part-time at first. Ellen worked on friends' properties and eventually got referrals from them and a local nursery.

Building and stewarding client relationships is something that Ellen did regularly as an attorney and this skill transferred well into her new business. She enjoyed the immediate connection with new clients and the process of developing a landscape plan to make them happier in their home environment.

Ellen thrives on creating gardens and landscapes that capture her clients' vision – whether it's recovering the beauty of an overgrown or ailing landscape or developing the possibilities of an empty space, transforming it from a detriment to an asset with a little attention. She creates themed gardens to respond to a client's interest, such as honoring a loved one, having a serene place to sit or meditate, or having an herb garden that provides outdoor interest and fragrance as well as bringing extra delight to cooking. She is a listener who partners with her clients to give them a way of reaching their goals whether they understand the green world or not.

The Weeds in a Workplace Garden

As her own boss, Ellen is thriving in an autonomous work environment where she can set high standards of excellence and have the freedom to create new services and products for clients. As an owner of a new business she admits the lack of security and endless demands on her time can be worrisome. But recognizing that she is now responsible for her success, and that she is not held back by being an employee for someone else, has proven tremendously liberating.

She encourages other women to think about what they really like to do and to not be deterred by the fear of not being able to make a living. Ellen suggests that career changers "...try it on and figure it out. There is a wonderful opportunity for trial and error and you can always change your mind. When you have created your new career the money will come."

Growing the Business

This budding entrepreneur (pun intended!) admits that watching expenses is always a concern. Her strategy is to keep overhead down and continue to build her clientele with excellent referrals and services that distinguish her from other landscape companies. Ellen learned early on that record keeping was a necessity and utilizes a variety of tools to manage her books, foster client communications, and facilitate marketing and networking.

Since gardening in Pennsylvania, where Ellen lives and works, is seasonal, she keeps busy in the winter months by taking classes and learning new techniques that will enhance her services to clients. She enrolled in the three-year certificate in horticulture program at the Barnes Foundation. "It is always fun to learn more and discover new possibilities in landscaping." Ellen also speaks to garden clubs and other groups giving presentations and demonstrations. She likes to plan new projects with clients so that they can start in the spring and she has launched a series of winter-proof indoor themed gardens that make wonderful presents for all occasions.

Marketing is always an important part of growing the business, no matter what the season. Ellen hired a marketing expert and recently launched a website that has given her a much needed online presence. She uses business cards with her new logo to network, and posts lawn signs at job locations to capitalize on curb appeal and drive-by prospective clients who see her work. She offers a free consultation as a way for her and a potential client to get to know one another and discuss the client's goals.

In 2010 the Wynnewood Business Association launched a recognition program for Women in Excellence and Ellen was the first recipient of its Women's Excellence in Business Award. She is very grateful for this award and sees it as a sign of growth as well as an incentive to continue to move forward with her company.

Garden Rehabilitator

Ellen has been landscaping since she was a child. She started her first garden with her mom in Connecticut and carries many of those techniques with her today. Gardening has also been a therapeutic outlet for Ellen, who found that immersing herself in it was a new way to create life when her marriage died. Gardening was cathartic and a healthy way for her to rebuild and renew her life.

Likewise, Ellen enjoys bringing diseased plants back to good health or moving an ailing plant to a better location in the landscape so it may provide renewed pleasure. Almost no specimens are beyond rehabilitation and with Ellen's expert knowledge and tender loving care, most plants come back to thrive in time.

Growth Potential

2010 marks four years for Ellen's business as a Limited Liability Company (LLC). She has steadily grown her clientele and works with a foreman and a crew who reflect the values of her company. She has built a collegial team that enjoys working together and loves what they do.

Using her lawyerly skills in problem solving, contracts, and project management, Ellen has built a business she loves. Since she traded in her corporate business suits for jeans, a sun hat and waterproof boots, Ellen enjoys wearing skirts and dresses when she is not at work. But there is nothing better for this lawyer turned landscaper than digging in the earth and creating custom gardens that bring delight to the senses.

Ellen's Advice and Action Steps:

- Take the time to figure out what you really love to do. Test-drive many things and know that you can always change your mind. You are not defined by your current occupation but have a diversity of talents and abilities within you.

• Never give up – what you are meant to do is out there somewhere waiting for you to discover it.

• Rally your support network (friends, family, additional resources) because you will need to lean on them during your transition.

• Don't be afraid to reinvent yourself – it can be very liberating.

Resources:

Custom Gardens, LLC: www.customgardensllc.com

❝Be as you wish to seem.❞

– Socrates

ભ ભ ભ ભ

23. TONYA FITZPATRICK: TURNING A PASSION FOR TRAVEL INTO A CAREER

Award-winning broadcaster and author Tonya Fitzpatrick always knew "come hell or high water" she would become a lawyer. She did just that, and enjoyed an appointment as a Deputy Assistant Secretary at the U.S. Department of Education, and also served under a federal defense contract as the Senior Legal Advisor for the Office of Civil Rights at the U.S. Department of Homeland Security. But her dissatisfaction with her legal career and the political environment in Washington, DC, confirmed that she was ready for a change. Traveling has always allowed Tonya to reconnect with herself; her passion for travel and a desire to live a purposeful life led her to reinvent her avocation and make it her career.

Wanderlust Leads to a New Career

This "recovering attorney" has stellar credentials that have empowered her with a myriad of transferable skills. Tonya graduated from the London School of Economics, East China University of Law and Politics, and Wayne State University Law School. She is also a student of the arts and previously worked at the Old Globe Theatre in San Diego and the Globe Theatre (under the late Sam Wannamaker) in London. According to Tonya, her greatest education has come through traveling – discovering different cultures, learning about the history, and meeting the beautiful citizens of the world. This is how she transitioned into her new role as a travel broadcast journalist, multimedia producer, and global citizen.

But how does one make the break from a secure legal career to making a livelihood traveling? According to Tonya, you honor your passion and the rest will follow. Tonya and her husband, Ian, also an attorney, left their law practices behind to create a unique global community through their travel radio show – *World Footprints* (formerly Travel'n On). Their decision to grow a community of fellow responsible travelers was affirmed when they were awarded the 2009 First Place Travel Broadcast from North American Travel Journalists Association. Since forming **Travel'n On Media Productions, LLC,** the producer of *World Footprints Radio*, they have expanded their broadcast platform to include additional multimedia digital platforms including internet, TV, and multiple social media platforms. This allows them to stay connected with their fellow travelers and grow their audience, even while on the road.

In addition to her role as Executive Producer of *World Footprints* and CEO of **Travel'n On Media Productions, LLC,** Tonya is also an author and speaker. She and Ian are currently writing a chapter in a book with Stephen Covey and they are producing new travel video content for major online media companies. Tonya also frequently covers travel-related legislation at the White House and Congress.

Planning for Change

Every move Tonya has made in life she has first carefully planned, and her exit from the legal profession was no exception. Her legal training helped her hone her research skills and she performs due diligence on every project she pursues. While she admits to being a risk taker, she also knows the importance of staying afloat financially. Tonya worked with a life/career coach to help her reinvent her passion for travel and turn it into a viable career. She also saved money to support herself for a full year, since she knew it would take time to turn a profit from the show and her new company.

The radio show makes money from investors, paid sponsors, and advertisers, but securing those has been a challenge in this tough economy. Tonya and Ian are now expanding their broadcast platforms and growing their audience by tapping into new markets such as university students who travel, study, and work abroad, and providing them with resources and a venue to share their experiences.

While Tonya is always using her transferable skills in contracts, negotiations, communication, and writing for the show and her company, she found it tough at first to "sell" her ideas and thought it would be easier to market someone else's product. But she has since overcome that feeling of insecurity and embraced her humble confidence in this project and the company that she truly believes in.

Celebrity Power on the Show

Prominent personalities and celebrity interviews on the radio show have given the program extra punch and increased the listening audience. Those special guests include actress and wildlife advocate Stefanie Powers, NASCAR icon Kyle Petty, philanthropist David Rockefeller, Jr., Rajmohan Gandhi (grandson of Mahatma Gandhi), Travel Channel hosts Samantha Brown, Andrew Zimmern, and Kirsten Gum, and many more celebrities and newsmakers.

World Footprints was granted accreditation to cover the 2010 Winter Olympics in Vancouver. Although some sporting events were covered, such as the Luge, Bobsled and Biathlon, the broadcast focus was on the cultural stories behind the games: how the First Nations people were represented, Vancouver's sustainable/green development legacy, and animal conservation efforts of the Olympic mascots. Tonya and Ian traveled to South Africa for the 2010 World Cup where, in addition to covering events and unique attractions, they also volunteered for a South African-based charitable organization that supports disadvantaged children.

An influential commentator, journalist, and thought leader in the travel arena, Tonya has been heard or seen on *MSNBC.com, NPR, Retirement Living, AllAfrica.com,* local CBS and NBC affiliate stations and others. Tonya is a member of the Society of American Travel Writers, the National Press Club, the North American Travel Journalist Association, and the Society of Professional Journalists. Both Tonya and Ian are members of the International Speakers Network.

Tonya and Ian are currently writing a chapter in a book entitled *Success Simplified,* with Stephen Covey, Patricia Fripp, and Tony Alessandra.

The Joy of Being Your Own Boss

The reality of being an entrepreneur is that you have total control over your business, and that you are solely responsible for your success or failure. Tonya has always had a strong work ethic and she believes it is now even stronger because she has taken ownership of her career future and her business. According to Tonya, she relies on her spiritual strength, prays a lot, and has created a work environment with Ian that values integrity, work ethic, and authenticity.

While Tonya's life has consisted of many exciting travel experiences, she has learned to take calculated risks and plan for them. She has lived, studied, and worked abroad in England, China, Russia, and Romania; her many travels have taken her through many regions of the world, including a five-week backpacking trip through Asia during which she returned to China and visited eight other countries in the region. As an avid scuba diver, she gravitates to coastal areas. She loves adventure and wants to trek through Nepal and climb Kilimanjaro someday soon.

But this adventurist has made a conscious effort to grow her business wisely instead of quickly, honoring the vision she and her husband have created.

From the beginning, responsible travel, culture, and heritage were values that Tonya and Ian brought to their show. *World Footprints* is unique in that its entire focus is about leaving positive footprints by fostering cross-cultural understanding and friendships, encouraging positive impacts on local people and their environments, supporting local trade and fair markets, and promoting authentic travel experiences that respect cultural heritage.

Tonya is on a quest to help others respect the natural environment and eco-balance of the planet by encouraging travel choices that minimize negative environmental impacts. One trip and one radio show or media product at a time, she and Ian are spreading their message, fulfilling their purpose, and living their dream.

Tonya's Advice and Action Steps:

- Honor your "red flags" and trust your gut.
- Grow your business wisely and not just quickly.
- Utilize your mentors and personal resource team.
- Be ready to pay-it-forward and help others.
- Be aware of your total skill set and tap into your strengths.

Resources:

World Footprints Media: www.WorldFootprints.com
International Speakers Network: www.bookaspeaker.net
Facebook World Footprints community: www.facebook.com/
  home.php#!/pages/WORLD-FOOTPRINTS-Media/272337714084
Twitter: www.twitter.com/WorldFootprints

❝Honor Your SELF and the rest will follow.❞

– Tonya Fitzpatrick

ல் ல் ல் ல்

24. BETH PATTERSON: LAW AND ENLIGHTENED ORDER

Beth Patterson has always been passionate about music, so her career progression from a boutique entertainment law firm, to RCA Records, and then to Elektra Entertainment were logical paths for this attorney after earning her JD from Brooklyn Law School. After the merger of AOL and Time Warner, Beth was laid off from Elektra and began to think seriously about her next career move. Ageism and sexism were alive and well in the corporate arena, according to Beth, so at 40-something she was ready to take her career into her own hands and make a change.

As a New Yorker who witnessed the second plane hit the World Trade Center on 9/11, she believes that this horrific event was also a catalyst that propelled her towards a change. Beth was with her husband in Vail, Colorado, attending a jazz music festival when they both fell in love with the idea of relocating and starting anew. Quite a bold decision for a native New Yorker who was not yet sure if there was life beyond the Big Apple.

A New Life Beckons

As a practicing Buddhist, Beth suffered through sexist bosses in the corporate arena who gave her additional grief for her enlightened spiritual ways. Colorado beckoned also because it is the home of Naropa University, a fully accredited Buddhist-oriented university, where Beth earned a Masters Degree in Transpersonal Counseling Psychology in 2006. She came to the conclusion that "...law just wasn't me anymore," and started on a personal journey at Naropa that ultimately led her to develop a private practice in psychotherapy and grief counseling in Denver, as well as a position as Life Care Coordinator for a Denver hospice.

Beth's studies at Naropa in human development in the second half of life allowed Beth to dig more deeply into her personal journey, and to develop her feminine self. Her life as a product of the Feminist Revolution did not accord with the traditional developmental model of Carl Jung, who had posited in his work during the Victorian Age that women in the second half of life worked to develop their masculine energy. One of her favorite books is Maureen Murdock's *The Heroine's Journey*, which details the passage women like Beth take in their quest towards wholeness in the second half of life, rediscovering their feminine energy that had to be suppressed to "make it" in the male-oriented corporate world.

A Jill of Three Trades

Beth is now enjoying a three-tiered career as a therapist in private practice, a Hospice bereavement and volunteer coordinator, and as a some-time attorney, representing musicians and other individuals in the arts. The foundation of her private practice is built upon the premise that a safe and non-judgmental therapeutic environment can help clients discover their innate inner resources in order to navigate life's inevitable changes, such as the death of a loved one or pet, divorce or separation, job loss, illness or disability, infertility, stressful caregiver trials or other life challenges.

"My therapeutic style is informed by my spiritual practice and deep belief that we all have the inherent wisdom to use our losses and other life challenges and transitions to grow and heal. My counseling practice is client-centered, grounded in wellness not sickness, and blends solution-focused, contemplative, body-centered and cognitive behavioral approaches."

In addition to her certification as a hospice trained grief counselor, Beth also practices EMDR (Eye Movement Desensitization and Reprocessing), an effective and scientifically proven tool for alleviating trauma, negative self-beliefs, chronic pain, depression, and anxiety by enhancing performance in all fields. A certified mindfulness meditation instructor, Beth has grown her professional skill set with these additional tools to empower her in her new career.

An Authentic Career Fit

This new career path comes as "such a relief" according to Beth, who is finally able to be herself in the workplace. She is also appreciated and acknowledged for her strengths and hard work, which she finds very rewarding. It was tough for Beth to leave the high salary security of corporate law in New York, but shedding the golden hand-cuffs was worth it in the long run for this legal counselor turned thera-pist. Beth shares an office with other practitioners to cut costs.

By nature, Beth is not a risk taker so the cross country relocation and career move was a leap of faith. She and her husband love the lifestyle in Colorado and her practice is on-the-grow. The cost of liv-ing is less than in New York, but she struggles with the health care system and dealing with insurance companies. As a solo practitioner, she does not accept insurance payments directly, but clients can sub-mit her bills for reimbursement if their plan includes mental health and wellness coverage. It's a challenge to help clients understand this process but she remains optimistic. Her goal is to have 10 steady cli-ents a week, in addition to her 30-hour a week hospice position, and to develop a strong referral system as her practice grows.

Breathing the mountain air of Denver has cleansed her body and soul and Beth is at peace with her transition. She reinvented herself career-wise and tapped into her inner woman to release a person who is passionate about helping others and in control of her happiness.

Beth's Advice and Action Steps:

- Don't beat yourself up – you need to be your number one advocate!
- Consider sharing office space until you can afford your own unique space.
- Be truthful with yourself. Listen to your heart and know what you are passionate about.
- Don't be afraid to be a woman – tap into your femininity.

Resources:

www.bethspatterson.com
www.bethspatterson.wordpress.com
Maureen Murdock's *The Heroine's Journey*

"Be a good person and be mindful
that your actions matter."

– Beth Patterson

ꝇ ꝇ ꝇ ꝇ

25. MARY WASIAK: BACK TO SCHOOL

Mary Wasiak was raised in a conservative family that always encouraged her to pursue a practical career. She always knew that she would attend graduate school but found herself in law school, without interest or aptitude for it, simply because it would lead to a sensible career. Little did she know that teaching would turn out to be her dream job in the near future.

It's Okay to Make a Career Change

Working full-time while in law school led to a much needed hiatus after her second year, and she returned to school older, wiser, and newly married to finish her law degree. With a focus on family law, property management, and contracts post-graduation, Mary found her legal career unfulfilling and sought other ways to play to her strengths. While she waited for her "aha" moment to happen in law, it never did, so she began to explore other options.

For three years she worked at Planned Parenthood doing outreach presentations in schools and she loved the rapport she built with the teenagers. She also worked for a Women's Advocacy Project serving women in small communities who were victims of domestic violence and teaching them how to represent themselves.

Mary conducted a myriad of informational interviews searching for a better career fit when one day her mother asked, "What do you love to do?" Mary responded, "I'm a teacher." And so this epiphany led Mary to apply for the Texas Teaching Fellows program.

Trading the Private Sector for Public Schools

The six-week intensive certification was part of a full year of instruction, observations, career counseling, and student teaching. Mary then flexed her newly honed teaching muscles through a placement with The New Teacher Project which matches teachers with schools in need. TNTP is highly competitive with an acceptance rate of only 15 percent and focuses on retraining career changers, so it was a perfect fit for Mary.

Mary now teaches in an ESL (English as a Second Language) classroom where the majority of her students are of Mexican or Hispanic origin. She also has one Taiwanese student. Her Spanish speaking skills have improved tremendously and Mary is pleased to be able to communicate effectively with her students and their parents. While a cacophony of languages is spoken regularly in her class, the emphasis is on English language acquisition.

Play to Your Strengths

Mary finds great value in her new career as a teacher where she can play to her strengths all the time, but admits the transition to teaching was a struggle. "I had to trust my instincts…" as the first six months proved to be a real challenge trying to figure out the right position within the new teaching realm.

As a teacher, Mary makes less than she would as an attorney, but you can't put a price tag on passion; what the job lacks in salary it replaces with benefits and security. But most of all, it is the realization that she is making a difference and serving the students that makes Mary content.

Many people envision the easy schedule of teachers with summers off and early afternoon quitting times but Mary says this is not always the case. She struggles with work/life balance in her new teaching role but she went in with her eyes open. With 7-, 10-, and 14-year-old children of her own at home, Mary has to be creative and energetic to keep up with the pace of her 50+ hour work week.

After a 9-hour work day, Mary often goes back to email at home in the evenings because the ESL program at her school is brand new and there is always room to do more. Yet Mary considers herself lucky in her new career as a teacher and tells her kids that, "Success is living the life that you want." This has turned out to be a family mantra for her household.

Award Winner

Mary has plans to stay at Crockett High School in Austin, Texas, for at least five years. She is learning so much on the job, and wants to stay to see that the changes she takes part in creating have a chance to be implemented. Her goal is to be a great teacher and perhaps work more on curriculum design and advisory lessons. Mary is certainly well on her way, for in 2009 she was awarded *Teacher of Promise*.

Mary's Advice and Action Steps:

- Trust your instincts and do what you love.
- Take the time to figure it out. Talk with everybody you know to learn about other career options.
- It's okay to retool or seek additional credentialing later in life.
- Lead with your strengths and you will be happy.

Resources:

The New Teacher Project www.tntp.org
Texas Teaching Fellows Program www.texasteachingfellows.org/

❝Success is living the life that you want.❞

– Mary Wasiak

ↄ ↄ ↄ ↄ

26. Take a Step Forward

Many people study law because they are interested in a profession. Throughout the ages, lawyers have enjoyed careers that focus on a call to serve, intellectual challenge, and growth opportunity that comes with financial gain. There are diverse practice areas, dynamic work environments, and prestige, to name just a few of the rewards of a legal career. Ellen Covner, Tonya Fitzpatrick, Beth Patterson, and Mary Wasiak needed more than these rewards to be gratified in their careers.

You Can Change Your Mind

For many who have spent a number of years in a given profession, it can be hard to let go and move on to new opportunities that better suit their passions and their values right now. I want you to erase the notion that you are *throwing away* one career for another when you make a change. Instead, think of yourself as a newly hatched butterfly ready for a fresh career journey. Giving yourself the freedom to understand that you can enjoy multiple careers in very different job sectors during your lifetime will liberate you to spend your time at work happy and fulfilled.

Often ego can get in the way of a career change. Our culture can ingrain in us the need to achieve a powerful rank or position that equates with career success. Some career changers don't want to let go of their elite position even if it makes them miserable because they worked so hard to get to where they are.

If your achievements don't echo what your heart and soul are feeling, then you are letting your ego get the better of you. Muster the courage to reinvent your professional identity and seek out help to explore new options. Dig deep to find a career that makes you joyful every day at work. Tap into the strengths that give you energy and satisfaction.

Can I Afford to Change Careers?

The reality is that we all need money to survive. But how much do you need to meet your needs, to make you happy, and to enjoy your life? Every person will have a unique answer to that question. Consider your relationship to money. Is it healthy and well balanced or do you have an addiction to acquiring things you *want* versus things you *need*?

It all comes back to values and how money plays a role in your life. If you prioritize financial wealth then you can certainly pursue a career that honors that value. But if you are transitioning to a new field or launching a new entrepreneurial venture, you may want to ease into the new opportunity so you can be prepared for the financial changes that may be ahead. Some of the women with whom I spoke kept a day job or worked at it part-time until their new business was financially solvent.

Have a plan and calculate what you really need to survive financially and how you want to utilize your savings (or not!) as you pursue a career change or new business. A career reinvention does not mean you have to move backwards financially, but you do need a plan so that you can make wise financial decisions.

REINVENTION TOOLBOX

Own Your Passion; Take Calculated Risks; Be Authentic

Earning a law degree takes an intense commitment, a large sum of money, and in most cases, three years of study. I applaud the self-described recovering lawyers in this chapter for taking a risk, owning their passion, and making authentic choices about why the legal profession was no longer for them.

Authenticity is the ability to be genuine and sincere with your intentions. All too often we make career decisions based on what others want us to do, or what we think they want us to do. Many of my clients and students have shared that they pursued *practical* professions because their families encouraged them to do so. While I believe families and support systems are important, ultimately the decision about career pursuits should be yours alone.

As the self-assessment process reveals, getting in touch with your values, interests, personality, and skills can help you discover career opportunities that truly match your authentic self. The realities of this job economy often force us to take stop-gap jobs in order to make ends meet, but never lose focus of your career dreams and continue to work towards those goals.

- How do you want to show up in the world?
- How do you want others to see you?

Most often, our personal and professional values are closely aligned. Have the courage to be true to yourself and trust your gut. The lawyers in this chapter took a risk leaving their solvent profession as attorneys and took a risk towards a more authentic career that honored their values.

The philosophical movement of existentialism has studied authenticity for centuries and helps us understand more about what authenticity is, along with its relationship to the concept of meaning. Existentialists assert that if an individual is not living authentically in their life, then they lose meaning and can fall into chronic anxiety, boredom, and despair. You spend a large portion of your waking hours on the job so you deserve to be happy in your career. Muster the courage to make authentic career choices that are meaningful to you. If you can align your values, talents, and vision, you can unleash a powerful trifecta that will lead you towards career satisfaction.

- Are you willing to take risks?
- Reflect on how you can move forward in your career by stepping outside your comfort zone and taking a risk.

When we meet successful people, we often mistakenly envy them for their great luck. Of course, their success has nothing to do with luck at all. Good fortune doesn't come to us; we go to it by taking risks. Life is all about taking risks.

And we willingly take chances every day. What separates achievers from ordinary folks is their willingness to take optional, as well as necessary, risks.

Without question, each of the 150 women I interviewed for this book took some form of risk and stepped outside their comfort zone as part of their career reinvention. Was it scary? Yes, but they grew and developed in ways that helped them succeed in the long run.

"Security is mostly a superstition. It does not exist in nature, nor do the children of men as a whole experience it. Avoiding danger is no safer in the long run than outright exposure. Life is either a daring adventure or nothing."

— Helen Keller

6

MAKE WAY FOR THE ARTISTS

A career transition doesn't always come from a place of unhappiness. Many of the artists in this chapter found new challenges to engage their passion or discovered new strengths by taking a career risk. Research shows that those with an artistic temperament are endowed with high levels of energy, self-confidence, sharp thinking, and humor, and often they assume leadership positions in their professions. That certainly describes these amazing women!

27. ANGELA JIA KIM: UNDERSTAND THE POWER OF AN ITCH

An accomplished concert pianist, Angela Jia Kim was about to step on stage when she developed an allergic reaction to a body lotion she had applied just before her performance. A consummate professional, she played the concert with her game face on and later discovered that the culprit lotion contained no less than 55 ingredients, most of which were chemicals. Most people would have simply searched for a new lotion, but most people are not Angela. Determined to create chemical- and preservative-free skin care made from organic ingredients, Angela set up shop in her New York City kitchen and experimented with all natural elements. She created a skin cream so delicious it was like food for your skin.

One Thousand Tries

Angela said it took over a thousand tries to perfect her skin cream before she was satisfied enough to give it to friends and family as gifts. The luxurious cream was an instant hit, but it was never meant to be a business (she meant only to create creams for herself and her loved ones); however, the passion developed organically as did the company. Friends were enthusiastic and shared samples with their friends and Angela's skin cream took off!

Angela began working with a team of holistic formulators, aromatherapists, and skin care experts, and **Om Aroma** was born. This line of skin care products is free of parabens, formaldehyde, mineral oil, and synthetic fragrances.

Soon after the company launch, **Om Aroma** won four gold medals at the 2008 Beauty Olympics, beating out some recognizable industry brands. All products are made in the USA and embody the fusion of luxury and organic. Angela's company is eco-friendly with packaging done by hand, using sustainable materials.

Angela is also committed to social responsibility, using fair-trade ingredients. Her *Dollars and Scents* program provides opportunities for women who are re-entering the work force and need a flexible work schedule due to having children, health issues, or a desire for a career change. **Om Aroma** products are never tested on animals.

Turning Problems into Opportunities

While growing her skin care business, Angela needed to also grow her professional network. Without any formal business training, she was in need of some "…nuts-and-bolts guidance, from launching to making millions," as she comments on her website. If a concert pianist, turned natural skin care guru is not amazing enough, you'll be pleased to know that Angela and her husband, Marc, also created **SavortheSuccess.com** – a boutique social network and PR Co-Op for female entrepreneurs and professionals.

SavortheSuccess.com is a tremendous resource that brings women together to share knowledge, expertise, resources and enthusiasm.

Transform Yourself

Angela is proof that women can transfer skills and switch career sectors. She turned a hobby into a thriving business and her passion, persistence, diligence, and strong work ethic transferred seamlessly into her new entrepreneurial venture.

Since hindsight is 20/20, Angela shared that if she had to do it all again, she would be more careful about choosing the people she hired. At first, she hired anyone who would work for her because she didn't know any better. But she soon learned the importance of being very selective so that you can surround yourself with an A-team that can propel the company to the next level.

As self-proclaimed skin care product junkie, I was eager to try **Om Aroma** and I can say that I am hooked. Not only do I use the products but I have found **SavortheSuccess.com** to be a tremendous resource which actually connected me to many of the fabulous women I have interviewed for my book.

Angela's Advice and Action Steps:

- Get rid of toxic people in your life – it drains your energy.
- Always try and recognize (from good and bad experiences) what works best for you.
- Identify what makes you, your service, or product special or unique. I call this the Chanel No. 5 factor. What is your Chanel No. 5 factor?
- Don't be afraid to ask for help. Surround yourself with supportive people and utilize resources. Follow your passion.
- Don't give up too soon. Try something multiple times before you throw in the towel. It took 100+ attempts to perfect my first batch of face cream.

Resources:

Om Aroma: www.omaroma.com
Savor the Success: www.savorthesuccess.com

> " It's all about how you play your game.
> Are you ready to *Savor the Success?* "

– Angela Jia Kim

✑ ✑ ✑ ✑

28. DANIELLE BOBISH: MAKING THE MOST OF YOUR CURTAIN CALL

A Broadway actress, Danielle was tired of being a struggling artist and knew she wanted more out of life and her career. But what – and how? Dissecting her career on the stage helped Danielle quickly realize that her professional theater background was the perfect training for planning large events. "With any big event like a wedding, you'll find the same key elements: costumes, lighting, set decoration, production and timing, and lots of details to coordinate. I thought – why not bring that same excitement and theatrical sensibility to non-Broadway events?" She is now the Owner and Creative Director of **Curtain Up Events (CUE)** and an excellent example of a woman who combined her passions, skills, and experiences and used them to transition into a new career.

Since 2005, Danielle has planned both intimate and large scale weddings and corporate events, including some of New York City's largest and most notable businesses. Located in the Big Apple, **Curtain Up Events** services the greater New York area but Danielle also travels out-of-state for destination events.

Use Self-Discovery for Career Transformation

She shared with me that she hit the wall as a performer and wanted self-validation as a person and not just as an actress. It was a vulnerable self-discovery process that helped her to realize that she was ready to leave the arts, and a very emotional decision. After many tears and a lot of deliberation about this major life and career change,

Danielle was ready to reinvent herself and moved forward with confidence and conviction.

As an actress, she had worked many a catering gig when not performing and since her Mom was a professional caterer, she grew up surrounded by people in the special events industry. After leaving show biz, Danielle developed phenomenal vendor contacts from a 2 ½ year stint at another event-planning firm where she worked prior to launching **CUE.** She received excellent reviews from colleagues and customers who encouraged her to set out her own shingle. Danielle combined her creative flair and business acumen to plan innovative and chic events under her new business name and thus, **Curtain Up Events** was born.

By the way, Madeline, Danielle's daughter was also born in 2009, and this working mom was producing events up until a week before she gave birth. She returned to work shortly after Madeline was born, but now does the logistical event planning from home to be closer to her daughter.

You Can't Move Forward Without Taking a Risk

Launching her own business was quite a risk, but Danielle is experiencing a validation that she finds very empowering. Her feedback from clients and vendors has been amazing and being her own boss has given her the freedom to make her own business decisions and to design her work schedule around raising a daughter.

As a proverbial Stage Manager, Danielle calls all the shots in her business and enjoys having the opportunity to work with fabulous people designing special events that make people joyful.

"If you've ever been backstage during a performance, there are so many things going on which keep the show running that the audience never sees. The same is true for a wedding. I'm calling a million different cues, but the guests just enjoy a seamless event. My musical-theater background also enables me to have a long list of theatrical vendors such as Tony-nominated lighting designers and Broadway performers that can make the day a little more spectacular.

Overall, I think the most unique thing I employ is my ability to connect with people. A wedding is a very personal event and all the special touches should reflect the couple and not me. Those special touches will make people say "that wedding was so THEM."

Her work and creative ideas appear on Brides.com, where she consults for numerous wedding planning stories. She was also a key producer on a team that planned an episode of "My Celebrity Wedding," which aired on The Style Network.

Balancing Act

The challenge for this working mom is balancing work with raising a daughter. Danielle wants to be an inspiration and a role model for her daughter but admits, "…sometimes you just have to budget to have someone watch the baby."

"My biggest challenge is balancing work and personal life. My daughter is very important to me and I constantly feel guilty about not spending enough time with her. I know that I really do give her everything she needs and then some. But you're always second guessing yourself and I'm always working at odd hours. There's always work to be done when you own your own company. Even if the clients are completely taken care of, you still have to tend to the company itself.

You really have to have an amazing support system. I have wonderful friends and family who are all hands on deck because they love me and believe in my company. I also have an AMAZING group of women who work with me. I couldn't do it without them and I tell them every chance I get. If you think you can do everything yourself, you'll just be running yourself ragged. It's so important to let others help you!!"

The curtain will rise and fall many times throughout our career lives. Danielle found her passion a second time and serves as an inspiration for others who are looking for that next career opportunity. She deserves a standing ovation!

Danielle's Advice

- Do what you love! I found something else I love, beyond my original career plan. I'm good at it and it makes me happy. Give yourself the opportunity to explore new things and find what you love.
- Take a risk – it could take you someplace wonderful.
- Be open to many things – you just might find something you never thought you would.
- Women can be competitive in the workplace so learn to work together and support each other and everybody wins.
- Always treat people with respect – sometimes it's contagious and that's a good thing.

Resources:

CUE: www.curtainupevents.com
Savor the Success: www.savorthesuccess.com

"I believe in the power of giving back and I have realized that you can't please everybody all the time.**"**

– Danielle Bobish

ॐ ॐ ॐ ॐ

29. GINGER HODGE: WHEN DONKEYS FLY

Born the youngest of five children in the small town of Sumter, South Carolina, Ginger Hodge was a bit shy as a child. With the love and support of her third-grade teacher, Ginger found the confidence to embrace her imagination and create unique ways to entertain herself and those around her. Those who know her best love that she always seems to have a new song, game, joke, or story to share.

Ginger landed her first job performing singing-balloon-a-grams while attending the College of Charleston. After graduation, she struggled to find her own way by dabbling with a few restaurant, real estate, and ad agency jobs. When she finally found her niche, in the movie industry, she was able to use her unique passion for entertaining others to market family-friendly films. But Ginger's true passion for living wasn't fully ignited until she published her first children's book: *When Donkeys Fly*.

What Will Your Epithet Say?

Looking back at how it all began, Ginger recalls waking up one morning after attending her uncle's funeral, worried that even if she were the very best at her job in the film industry, her epithet would read: "Best B Movie Buyer in the Business" – and that just wasn't enough. As a senior "blurbologist" (her own unique term), she wrote the copy on the back of DVDs/videos, scouted new producers, and licensed family films to be sold at retail.

After learning of all the wonderful ways her uncle gave back to the community during his lifetime, Ginger decided then and there that she wanted to make a difference in the world and began indulging her true passion – writing. She wrote *When Donkeys Fly*, left her six-figure career in what she called the "gloom and doom entertainment industry," and embarked on a mission to lead, and encourage others to lead, an extraordinary life.

When Donkeys Fly is an inspirational book for all ages that encourages people to believe in themselves despite any obstacles. *When Donkeys Fly* won the Mom's Choice Award® for "Most Inspirational/Motivational" new book, and this is the message she is on a quest to share with anyone who will listen.

Ginger and her faithful flying donkey travel to schools, churches, colleges, and women's groups all over the country to read the book, sing a song, and encourage other donkeys to fly.

Flying without a Net

In the spirit of the book, Ginger and a friend started a band called "Cosmo and the Flying Donkeys" to encourage other music lovers to follow their own passions. But how does one walk away from a financially secure job and start a new career as a first-time author or musician and make ends meet?

This new author took advantage of the growing self-publishing movement and borrowed against the equity in her home to finance the book and launch her new career.

This leap of faith was incredibly scary but also invigorating for Ginger who, for the first time, was flying without the proverbial safety net. The ability to shed corporate policy for personal satisfaction was very liberating for Ginger, who is now relieved to be able to speak her own truth.

She recalls being on pins and needles in the film industry – much of the time living and working in a stress-based environment. Now, as her own boss, she can spend the afternoon playing with her niece, walking the beach, or taking her dad to the doctor because she is in charge of her own time.

Quality of Life

Even though she can't count on a regular paycheck every Friday, Ginger believes that her lifestyle has changed for the better. For the first time in years, she can literally taste and enjoy the food she eats and not have to wolf down meals to make the next meeting or deadline. Ginger has embraced a life of "living in the moment" and appreciates the simple pleasures more than ever.

> "I knew that I made the right decision when I had my first massage after leaving the entertainment industry. After a few minutes of massage, my magical masseuse was surprised to find that the 'stress knots' she routinely battled in my back were gone. Who knows how many years I have added to my life by choosing to follow my heart instead of my wallet."

Ginger reports that financially things are going well and although she is not making what she did in the film industry (yet!), she is happy because she is living her values and following her passion, and you can't put a price tag on that. She encourages others to follow their hearts; and that is the premise of her book.

In addition to the book, donkeys are flying through classrooms with the help of Ginger's techno-savvy sister who developed a series of activities and resources for collaborative technology and literacy integration projects. Using Skype and Voicethread, kids can instantly

connect with the characters and the events in the story. Student
joy the rhythm of the text and the captivating illustrations and can
even connect with Ginger directly through www.skypeanauthor.com.
Ginger is thrilled to be able to find new ways to share the positive
message of the book with children all over the world and maintains a
blog – Friends of the Flying Donkey – where she shares moving stories of her adventures in the classroom and beyond.

Here is a letter that was forwarded from a first-grade teacher after
one of Ginger's school presentations:

"I think Ms. Hodge did a wonderful job! One child in my class
had struggled drawing a picture of herself yesterday so I asked her to
finish it today. She did a wonderful job and as I bragged on her, she
stated, 'I just let my donkey fly.'"

The Mission

Ginger is on a personal mission to improve self-esteem and literacy in schools. For younger students, she reads her book, sings her
song, and walks kids through the publishing process with a message that will boost self-confidence and creativity. For high school
students, she adapts the message to focus on career development with
practical tips to follow their dreams to the job market.

Ginger's Flying Donkey team also has plans to further promote literacy by recruiting college and semi-pro athletes to go to schools, read
the book to the students, and share stories of how their own donkeys
learned to fly.

According to Ginger:

"It has been statistically shown that students whose reading
scores are below the national average in third grade rarely ever
catch back up, so our goal is to share the positive message
of *When Donkeys Fly* with every third-grade student. And
South Carolina is only the beginning....

For students to learn to read, they first have to believe it is
possible, right? Our goal is to take literacy to a higher level
by encouraging kids to believe that they can do anything, including excel at reading despite their own circumstances or
previous test rankings.

To date, we have a commitment from The Carolina Game-cocks, interest from The Citadel Bulldogs, The Charleston River Dogs, The Florence Red Wolves, and yes, even a few Roller Derby teams... and this is only the beginning!"

Donkey Power

The charming book assures girls and boys everywhere that their dreams can come true. Several scenarios describe how people scoff at the heroine's hopes to play baseball, to own a big boat, to be President of the United States, etc., by saying "You'll do that...when donkeys fly." Then one day she spots a flying donkey and realizes that all things are possible.

The book has an added challenge of hunting for the hidden donkey in the illustration on each page. And the "Note from the Author" in the back of the book reveals the deeper, more spiritual, message of the hidden donkey for those who wish to find it.

Although *When Donkeys Fly* is a child-friendly book, it can also be the perfect gift for graduation, birthday, or any holiday for the special people in your circle of friends and family.

After growing up in the direct-to-retail world of the film industry, Ginger's transferable skills and experience were very applicable when the time came to market her book. She attends national conferences and speaks to groups from kindergarten classes to national professional organizations.

In fact, *When Donkeys Fly* was chosen by Executive Women International (EWI) as the book featured at their National Reading Rally. When asked about her finest hour as an author, Ginger recalls the looks on the faces of the students chosen from Louisville, Kentucky to be honored guests of EWI. As they entered the convention center, pages of the book were blown up bigger than life, animated donkeys flew across 30-foot screens, and over 600 executives gave a rousing standing ovation as the music played from a special rendition of "I Believe I Can Fly." Anyone could tell, simply from their expressions, that these students from one of the most poverty-stricken schools in the state believed that anything was possible...when donkeys fly.

Everything Happens for a Reason

Ginger doesn't take full credit for writing the book and believes that the book was simply a gift that was meant to be shared. The day the ideas came to her, Ginger literally pulled her car over to the side of the road and remembers the words coming to her faster than she could write. She wrote the entire book in less than seven minutes, but feels that the ideas for it must have been "baking" in her mind for years.

Once written, Ginger sent an email to all of her college friends who now have children, to get their reactions to the story. Soon after the email, her friend C.B. Markham answered and said "I love the story so much I am going to illustrate this book… just for me." Long story short, Ginger loved her illustrations and the power of *seek and you will find* was confirmed.

Ginger has plans in the works for her own publishing company, **Donkey Fly Press** and has two other books in the pipeline: *When I Get a Dog* and *When Pigs Fly*. She has taken stock of what is important in her life and made sacrifices to follow her passion. After the initial shock of job separation, she is now at peace with her decision and has made it her mission to help children and adults overcome obstacles, achieve empowerment, embrace their self-confidence and follow their own flying donkeys.

Ginger still lives in South Carolina with her faithful Labrador, Sadie, and her boat "Mr. Right."

Ginger's Advice and Action Steps:

- Set your intentions.
- Follow your passions.
- Savor every moment.
- Don't let money drive your decisions.
- Strive to be peaceful and productive.
- Help those who help others.
- Remember that everything happens in divine time.

Resources:

When Donkeys Fly: www.whendonkeysflybook.com

> "Take a moral inventory of what success means
> to you – really think about it! Everyone can sing –
> you've just got to find your song."

> – Ginger Hodge

ℱ ℱ ℱ ℱ

30. Jo Laurie: Do You Live To Work or Work to Live?

Quintessential Jill-of-all-trades, Jo Laurie has experienced many career changes in her life. As a young student in her native England, Jo was pushed into the empirical sciences in school and specialized early on in chemistry, physics, and math. She is dyslexic and these disciplines were meant to help her focus on her strengths with numbers and equations.

Jo was successful in the sciences and in the British system under Margaret Thatcher; she was paid to attend university (free tuition plus a stipend) and earned a BSc (Hons), a degree with honors in Psychology. While Jo was stimulated intellectually, she yearned for a more creative outlet. So she left England and headed to New York City to reinvent herself and test-drive a new world.

Millinery Mania

For two years she explored her artistic side, working a total of 17 different jobs from modeling to jewelry making and restaurant work. She taught herself how to cook and sew and she discovered a passion for making hats. Her millinery creations took off and Jo hit the big time when her hats were picked up by the exclusive three Bs department stores in New York City: Barney's, Bergdorf Goodman and Henri Bendel, and soon after, 70 stores worldwide.

While the hat business was successful for a good while, Jo's artistic wanderlust led her to try additional opportunities, styling props and creating environments for photographers. In her bones she knew that she did not enjoy working for other people in a corporate or structured environment. She longed to be her own boss and match her creative talents with her scientific skill set. Friends asked her to consider designing a bar for them back in London and that was the beginning of **Jo Laurie Interior Design**.

Values of a Dual Citizen

Jo enjoys the best of her American and English worlds as a dual citizen and her design firm is home based in the USA to capitalize on the significance of New York City on the global stage. She shared with me her frustration about the American system of a typical two-week vacation allotment for most employees in an organization and thus, she really values being in control of her own time as her own boss.

This globe-trotter doesn't *live to work* but *works to live*. She subscribes to the continental work philosophy of enjoying six-plus weeks of vacation annually. This is the norm in Europe, Australia and Canada but it saddens Jo that most American companies offer only a paltry two-week vacation period. There has been significant research that indicates European executives are more industrious per hour, as they are more rested mentally and physically. This translates into better productivity on the job. Jo is in touch with what she values and has made priorities in her life accordingly to live these principles.

The Reality of Being Your Own Boss

Jo has come a long way from her millinery days and established a multi-discipline design company, with projects ranging from corporate and hospitality to high-end residential. Located in downtown Manhattan, she has been operating internationally for over 15 years, and has developed an extensive portfolio of award-winning projects. As an interior designer, she has developed an understanding of the specialized needs of her clients worldwide by creating visually stimulating surroundings that produce unique, flexible, and functional environments.

But success does not come easily and even though Jo prioritizes multiple-week vacations each year, she works around the clock to keep her business thriving. Ninety-five percent of her business comes from referrals and satisfied customers. Her website is a powerful marketing tool and offers a delicious taste of the types of interiors Jo has created.

Her personal Board of Directors includes an old friend who has a very successful architecture firm who helps Jo navigate the business side of interior design. This mentorship has helped Jo identify and market her special sauce in the design arena. Another friend developed her website, brand, and identity. Her team is rounded out by an accountant, a marketing specialist, and another friend who has achieved great success in the financial industry. Jo has assembled a great resource team.

Dollars and Sense

While Jo is flexing her artistic muscles, she must always be concerned about the nuts and bolts of the business. Like many creative individuals, her first passion is the creative process, which in itself was not initiated by the desire to make money. With the help of some good mentors, Jo has seen a steady increase in clients as the businesses continue to grow – even in the recession. Cultivating new business is a constant need, so she also adheres to a realistic budget and a business framework that keeps her in the black.

The recession has hit the design industry as a whole, and for Jo, it has made cultivating new business more important than ever. She is always prepared to take a risk and try new things to make her business viable. Inspired by her grandmother, who always told Jo to go for it, she believes that taking a risk forces you to go to the next level. According to Jo, "You must continue to take risks to build your business and your dream. When you fail, you pick yourself up and start again because that's what it's all about."

The Belle of the Bar

While Jo has achieved international recognition for her pub and bar interior designs from Sydney to London and beyond, she remains grounded in what is important to her. Personal life situations have helped Jo put it all in perspective, keep her focus on what is important in life, and to truly live what she values.

Jo continues to travel internationally to build her clientele and her inspiration for new designs. This straight-talking modern English-woman, whose formal education is steeped in the empirical sciences, has found a way to blend form, function, and art to build a business that meets her values and her passion. I have every confidence that Jo will continue to grow her career in different directions because blended within her inner scientist is the true temperament of an artist.

Jo's Advice and Action Steps:

- Unorthodox is good – don't be afraid to be different.
- Get other people to do what you can't so you can concentrate on what you love and what you do well.
- Develop a resource team of experts to rely on when you need assistance. It's a worthy investment.

Resources:

Jo Laurie Design: www.jolauriedesign.com
Savor the Success: www.savorthesuccess.com/member/jo_laurie
www.linkedin.com/in/jolauriedesign
www.upworld.com/jolauriedesign

66Your generation of women should do
because you can!99

– Jo's Grandmother

ᑲ ᑲ ᑲ ᑲ

31. Take a Step Forward

Throughout the journey of interviewing 150+ women for my book and blog project, I have met people with infectious positive attitudes. Angela Jia Kim, Danielle Bobish, Ginger Hodge and Jo Laurie are great examples of women who have created careers they can live with positive energy. Not only are they flourishing in their professions, they are paying-it-forward to help others, and savoring each moment of their success.

Be Accountable

The truth is that you alone are responsible for your personal and professional growth. No company, boss, or mentor is on a mission to create your perfect work environment. The buck stops with you and you owe it to yourself to take control of your future. It begins with a critical self-assessment of your values, interests, personality and skills and moves forward with your motivation and ability to devise an action plan.

If you don't like the way you are feeling, the quickest and most effective way to change is to adjust your thinking. Do everything in your power to achieve a positive and optimistic attitude. Employers have confirmed that attitude is more important than education and skills. You can learn new skills but if you don't bring a positive attitude to the table, you are selling yourself short.

Positive attitude affects your day-to-day performance and plays a role in every aspect of your life. The way you envision your career and your life is the way you will live it. Remove toxic people from your daily life and surround yourself with people who share your positive and buoyant outlook. Positivity is infectious and you will reach your goals faster if you are living and working in a constructive environment with a support system that is cheering you on to achieve your goals.

Savor Each Moment

Angela Jia Kim has built her business, **SavortheSuccess.com** on the philosophy that you should relish every moment of success as you work towards your goals. Our education system is predicated on helping students improve by showing them what they did wrong. Do you remember the big red X on your childhood tests indicating an incorrect answer? How sad that we were not commended for the questions we answered correctly; the focus was always on what we needed to improve.

I urge you to focus on the positive and learn to showcase what you do well. You are not broken; if you take the time to play to your strengths instead of always trying to fix your weaknesses, you will be much happier. Savor what you do well and relish the small things each day that make you smile. Literally stop to smell the roses and focus on what you really need to bring you satisfaction.

Often we are so busy working that we don't enjoy living. Take a tip from Jo Laurie and *work to live* as opposed to living to work, so you can enjoy your life in addition to your profession and have more time to do what you really love outside of work.

REINVENTION TOOLBOX

Recognize Your Transferable Skills; Develop Your Professional Poise; Give-Give-Get

As a fellow artist, I can truly relate to the women in this chapter. My colleagues refer to me as the *Queen of Transferable Skills* because I have learned the broad spectrum of skills I possess and I now know how to tell others what I do well.

Ideally, I want you to tap into the skills that give you strength. I happen to clean my house very well – that is a skill. But it's not a skill that gives me strength or one that I choose to utilize in my career pursuits.

- What are the skills in your repertoire that give you strength? Write down at least three.
- What tasks energize you and leave you wanting to do more? Add to the list as you discover new tasks.

I want you to think about the kinds of things you enjoy doing so much that you can actually lose track of time while doing them. These are the skills that you probably enjoy using the most. They are transferable because you can use them in any career field that you choose which needs that skill set.

Start your career reinvention research focusing on the skills that bring you strength. Don't think about job titles or industries yet. First, identify what you really enjoy doing and then research ways that you can employ these skills in a career.

Don't confuse transferable skills with traits like: *dependable*, *works well under pressure*, and *has a great work ethic*. These are traits and, though important, it is the skills that you are first selling to a prospective employer. Be ready to tell your skills story as you network and pursue research about new career opportunities. Eventually, you will share your skills story in a job interview.

A client of mine identified her top skill as *organizing* but her story fell flat because she did not flesh out exactly what she liked to organize. After some coaching, and a full-scale reflection about her organizing experiences, she developed a more effective narrative. She was able to articulate that she organized people, ideas, and events and was able to take brainstorming sessions from the board room to full-scale implementation working with vendors, staff, donors, and volunteers. She landed a position as an Events Coordinator in a nonprofit organization and is happily playing to her organizational strengths.

Do you have Stage Presence?

As an opera singer, I know from experience that stage presence speaks volumes about how you are perceived. The audience forms an impression of you before you even open your mouth, and the same rings true in the world-of-work. You have control over the way you carry and comport yourself and these traits can help you own your self-confidence.

Here are some quick strategies to ramp up your professional poise:

- **Stand tall and use good posture** when sitting in a board meeting, making a presentation, or even grabbing coffee in the company break room. Good posture is healthy, conveys confidence, and can make you look five pounds thinner (that's my kind of diet!).

- **Analyze your speaking voice.** Be sure to speak slowly, clearly, and keep your volume constant throughout your statements. Use proper grammar and work towards eliminating filler phrases such as: *like, um* and *you know*.

- **Dress the part.** Take stock of your professional wardrobe and make sure you are neatly groomed and wearing clothing that reflects the culture (and decade!) of your work environment. Ill-fitting and sloppy clothing sends an immediate negative message to your clients and colleagues.

- **Have a positive attitude and avoid work place gossip and politics.** Positivity is infectious and can impact how you perform on the job. Pay-it-forward with an upbeat mindset and watch your colleagues follow suit.

- **Be mindful of the rules of etiquette** whether you are hosting a client for a business lunch or a guest at your boss's holiday party. Retool your etiquette know-how so that you can be comfortable eating and socializing in a professional environment.

Giving Back

I formed my singing group *The Grateful Divas* so I could use my musical talent to give back to nonprofit and charitable organizations and because I still love to perform. By helping these groups raise money and awareness, I am making a contribution to institutions I believe in.

So many of the women profiled in this book have incorporated ways to give back in their businesses and private lives. Whether it is volunteering your time and expertise or donating a percentage of targeted proceeds towards a worthy cause, generosity and the spirit of community are being celebrated on a grand scale.

In an era when business ethics have been questionable in our world, what better way to teach the children of the next generation that philanthropy matters than by paying-it-forward?

- How will you share your time, talents or treasure in your community?
- Give yourself a 90-day window to do your research and implement your give-back plan.

Considering how you can help others will increase your personal capital. Careers are a lifelong journey and we've all had people that were instrumental in helping us along the way in good times and in bad. Make an effort to be conscious about how you are helping others because what goes around really does come around.

7

LET'S HEAR IT FOR THE WAHMS: WORK-AT-HOME MOMS

Work-at-home moms, or WAHMs, are on the job 24/7. While working from home may seem like a luxury, it is also the definition of multitasking and flexibility. These amazing moms are nurturing their careers and families, as well as themselves.

32. VIANESA VARGAS: FIRST, TAKE CARE OF YOURSELF

With ten years of active duty service under her belt, Vianesa Vargas was on track to be a commander in the military. But after the birth of her second son, she was given orders to serve in Iraq for another year plus three additional months of training. It was then that she decided to leave the Air Force and pursue her other call-to-serve, to help women be the best moms they can be and to lead confident, fulfilling lives.

Vianesa (or V, as her friends call her) spoke to many military career women who were also struggling with the question of whether to serve themselves and their families first, or their careers. With four deployments to the Middle East already under her belt, Vianesa knew her personal decision to leave the military was one that she could pursue without regrets. She does admit that leaving was not without guilt but when she finally came to terms with the fact that her guilt was self-imposed, she was able to move on and embrace her new career dreams and goals.

Living a Guilt Free Life

Her new mission is to show other busy moms how they can make time for their families, work, passions, and most importantly, themselves. Vianesa founded the **Take Care Project**, an online health and wellness resource for busy moms. She is also a wellness coach and the author of an exercise and nutrition journal, written expressly for women who are struggling to juggle motherhood and their diet and exercise goals.

"The products I launched are tailored to a mom's wellness. I listen to my market and create products to fulfill their needs. Casual t-shirts and the exercise journal are available now. We're also planning to launch a toolkit for moms who are struggling with the transition to motherhood as well as an exercise book for new moms."

Although Vianesa is proud of her country and her military career accomplishments, her most rewarding experience is that of becoming a wife to a loving husband and mother to two wonderful boys.

"I know all too well how much of an experience it is to bring a child into this world and then to watch this *experiment* grow into what you shape it. The demands of motherhood on your body and mind can be intense, but the **Take Care Project** will be with you along the way. My purpose is to give mothers the resources needed to take care of themselves FIRST!"

Honoring Your Body

Long before her military career, Vianesa learned how to get into tip-top physical shape and she enjoys maintaining this healthy lifestyle even now as a civilian. With degrees in biology and nutrition studies, Vianesa has developed simple and easy-to-remember strategies that mothers can use to improve their own health and wellness.

While she was ready to transition to a new career, post-military, Vianesa says the Air Force provided her with some excellent transferable skills. She is flexible, able to adapt quickly to change, and knows how to prioritize tasks. Vianesa's Air Force career also afforded her financial stability and with her dedicated savings plan, she was able to sock away money over the years that gave her the nest egg to finance her new business venture.

But how do you transition from the military to launch a national online business for moms? Vianesa was a faithful reader of *Entrepreneur Magazine* and also utilized SCORE (Counselors to America's Small Business) advisors in her community. She hired a web designer and built her business with the support and enthusiasm of her husband who shares in her vision to help others. The goal is to build a wellness company that empowers working moms with resources, products, and inspiration. Long-term, Vianesa plans to open a wellness center and after talking with her, I am confident that she will make this goal a reality. But every career has challenges and Vianesa was candid while sharing hers.

> "A challenge is finding the time to effectively manage a business start-up. It is extremely important for women to continue to exercise, eat right and rest, as I can attest to. I have made several mistakes by working all day, raising children, and then having to work on my business. You are more effective when healthy and well rested."

Look to Your Communities

The military taught Vianesa how to be resourceful and the **Take Care Project** shows women how to do the same. Vianesa encourages moms to find a support system in their communities. Look for mentors and seek out shared services like child care and carpooling to simplify your challenges. The messages of **Take Care Project** focus on health, spirit, fun, fitness, rest, and green living. Vianesa's site features thoughtful and inspiring articles as well as a blog to help mothers achieve their personal goals, at their own pace.

While Vianesa was on her way to breaking through the glass ceiling in the military, she values her new career even more because it feeds her passion. Look for Vianesa on the national circuit as a motivational speaker and writer in publications such as *Essence*, *Working Mother*, *Heart & Soul*, and *Family* magazines and check out **Take Care Project** online.

Vianesa's Advice and Action Steps:

- Get clear and focused about why you want to start a business.
- Get mentored and listen to those who have already done what you're trying to do. Become a student of the trade so to speak, and read, read, read!
- Make it happen by getting a business plan written and decide if it is a worthwhile venture. If not, go back to the drawing board.

Resources:

Take Care Project: www.takecareproject.com
Entrepreneur Magazine
SCORE: www.score.org

66Excellence is what we repeatedly do. Excellence is not an act but a habit.99

– Aristotle

ↂ ↂ ↂ ↂ

33. PAM BEATTIE: FRIENDLY FUR LEADS TO A BUSINESS WITH REPURPOSE

When Pam Beattie, a stay-at-home mom, and married for 20 years, had a yearning for something more, she focused on her passion for French furniture to launch a new business. **Venetian Décor** is her boutique upholstery and design house that specializes in creating down duvets, custom filled seat cushions and reproduction French furniture, to name just a few of her offerings. Pam is the ultimate recycler using vintage fur coats to bring a new life to these heirlooms and repurpose them for something new and unique.

Pam designs custom pieces that act as windows in time and reflect old world craftsmanship, dedication, and attention to detail. **Venetian Décor** does not promote the trapping and killing of animals, but works exclusively with vintage fur coats to ensure that these historic resources are refashioned into useful and appreciated products.

According to Pam:

"Our mission is to imbue a little corner of your life with some old-world magic and elegance by repurposing vintage items and giving them a modern twist. My love of beautiful vintage fur coats and French furniture inspired me to create this line of products for you to enjoy for many years to come."

A Little Bit of History Preserved

Her signature pieces are beautiful one-of-a-kind furnishings and throws made from vintage fur coats and buttons just like great-grandmother owned. "We are based in the Coast Mountains of British Columbia, where the pioneer spirit of early fur trappers and adventurers still whispers through the spruce and fir at night, and the hopes of gold-seekers echo down the wild rivers." For Pam, working with repurposed fur coats and vintage rhinestone buttons and jewelry is a chance to imagine a moment in time in a world of horse-drawn buggies and mink capes to bring a touch of old-world elegance into the busy modern world.

Pam came up with the prototypes for **Venetian Décor** in her home studio, an 800-square-foot space where she also sells her creations. She uses Italian-made and imported French furniture as well as antique French furniture for her pieces. The soft Italian-made leathers, natural silk fabrics and ribbons, plus natural down cushions and wool are the ultimate in eco friendly materials.

Her first big break came from an Interior Design Show in Vancouver, British Columbia, where she showcased her wares. A writer profiled her business and featured a two-page article in the *Vancouver Sun* newspaper with photos, and the official buzz began. The writer tackled the animal rights issue and deftly wrote that repurposed fur means that no animals have died today. It also means that no faux fur, with its own environmental issues including pollution and petroleum-based synthetics are being manufactured for these artistic creations.

Pam has her own philosophy about using vintage fur:

"I truly believe that I have found a final resting place for these animals. It's a way to say that we appreciate you and respect you."

Whether you believe in Pam's vintage fur credo or not, kudos are due to this *mompreneur* who has created a viable business she is passionate about.

Venetian Décor was featured in a high-profile article in the *Beverly Hills Times* magazine. Pam hopes this will introduce her brand to celebrity clientele who could really put her on the map. The **Venetian Décor** signature style is a blending of shabby-chic, eco-chic, French, Boho, and refined but relaxed glamour styles, blended together for a one-of-a kind design.

The Challenges of a Working Mother

Inspired by her own creative mother who was a ceramics artist, Pam feels a great sense of accomplishment with her new business venture. She still loves being a mother but finds this new work fulfilling, and it gives her a sense of purpose so that she can now put herself first. Her husband and family have been very supportive and enthusiastic and her daughters even lend a hand with her pieces.

With a new beginning in her 40s as her kids are about to leave the nest, Pam is ready to succeed in her new business but admits there are challenges. She is a one-woman show and shared that her responsibilities as a wife and mother don't change with her new business, so now she has two full-time jobs!

Without financial backing or business loans available to her, Pam used her savings to purchase the start-up materials including reproduction furniture from Italy. She reinvests her profit into the business and keeps her overhead low by working from her home studio. Her husband is a professional in the building industry so he has been helpful as a resource for some basic business fundamentals, but Pam has been on her own to learn the trade of the interior design industry. She advises other budding entrepreneurs to do their research about trademark, company name and logo first, and then focus on your product.

Waste Not, Want Not

Inspired by *shabby chic* queen, Rachel Ashwell, Pam is building her brand on the historic preservation of vintage furs as a way to honor the history of each piece with a new life. Repurposing has become vogue in the art, interior design, and fashion worlds so Pam is capitalizing on the "waste not, want not" approach. Since vintage fur can last up to 100 years, her creations make sustainable sense economically, environmentally, and socially.

Pam was featured on the Canadian TV show *Urban Rush* and she was recently approached by a jewelry designer to sell her pieces in their store. These baubles are a favorite of celebrities Tori Spelling and Anne Heche, so Pam hopes that the women might also consider buying one of her pieces. If you have an heirloom fur coat that you want repurposed, consider commissioning Pam to make you a custom piece that will live on for years to come.

While Pam is living a new dream with her own business, she is also establishing a practice of repurposing and recycling items to create new furnishings. This businesswoman with a conscience feels like a butterfly that has just begun to spread her new wings.

Pam's Advice and Action Steps:

- Don't overwhelm yourself with a new business, take baby steps and preserve your inner peace.
- Follow your heart and do something you are passionate about.
- Be sure you have a good resource team (family, mentors, etc.) to back you up.
- Go for it because you have nothing to lose by trying.
- Do your homework in setting up your trademark, company name and logo.

Resources:

Venetian Décor: www.venentiandecor.com
Fur Council: www.furcouncil.com

"You will never know if you don't try."

– Pam Beattie

ᔕ ᔕ ᔕ ᔕ

34. CANDACE ALPER: NAME YOUR TUNE

It all began for Candace Alper when she was on maternity leave. In Canada, new moms are able to take up to a year off which has led to a growing number of *mompreneurs* in the country. Having a year to herself and her new baby, Candace was able to take the time to think about her life and her career. With an infant daughter, she started singing the songs all moms know and love, but she would incorporate Hannah's name to personalize the tunes.

Before long, "If You're Happy and You Know It" became "If You're Hannah and You Know It," and the idea of **Name Your Tune** was born. Candace's husband, Eric, works in the music industry and he supported the idea of the new business venture and also brought significant skills and expertise to the table. From the beginning, the focus has been on making music fun for children and parents alike. By customizing songs with a child's name, this wife and husband team has been able to take classic children's songs to a new place.

Sing a New Song

Candace admittedly has no experience in the music industry, but her background in liberal arts and education has provided her with a cadre of transferable skills that help her run the business. Directly after college, Candace hoped to pursue teaching but the lack of opportunities in the education field led her to a position in the retail industry. She was working her way up the management ladder when she became pregnant with Hannah. The plan was to go back right after her maternity leave, but **Name Your Tune** happily took her life in a different direction.

Candace has been active with children and youth in her community through social programs, summer camps, and trips abroad, so creating a new business about kids was an ideal fit. They started with nine songs and eight hundred recorded names. Candace and Eric invented the technology to personalize the songs with a child's name in the recording process.

Eric's music background came in very handy with this new business venture. As the company cofounder, he has been active in the Canadian music scene for 15+ years and has experience with media relations and acquisitions for Koch Entertainment, which proved extremely valuable for **Name Your Tune**.

Bringing Home the Bacon and Cooking It

In the beginning, Candace admits she was useless around computers as technology was not her forte. But she is now the company's one-woman IT department and coordinates the efforts of four amazing singers, producers, and a West Coast office, handling most of the day-to-day tasks herself.

Being a *mompreneur* and a WAHM (work-at-home mom) means that Candace can be her own boss. She sets her own hours, which lends itself to a flexible schedule so that she can balance her varying roles as a mom, wife, daughter, sister, and business owner. While Candace admits to accepting a certain amount of imbalance as a reality to her day, she feels fortunate to be able to work from home and enjoy the little things that she couldn't do if she worked off-site.

While juggling **Name Your Tune** responsibilities she usually does a few loads of laundry and gets her daughter to and from school daily. She has become the queen of multitasking. On an ambitious day this might also include cooking a batch of homemade spaghetti sauce because these are things that she is able to fit into her work day now.

A Hard Day's Night

While the work day might sound idyllic, prioritizing her family during the day means that Candace often works at the computer well into the night. Eric is often at her side since this business is truly a joint venture and a family affair. She has his total support and kid coverage when the job requires her working weekends away for promotional events to brand their product. They have developed a partnership and have each other's backs to cover things on the work and home front.

Since the company launch, **Name Your Tune** has become the leading personalized CD in the world. Children will hear their name more than 80 times throughout 14 treasured songs and they now have over 4500 names to choose from!

People Magazine called **Name Your Tune** CDs, "This year's most coveted item," in 2009. NBC's *The Today Show* calls the CD, "Must have baby gear – now that's something to sing about!" Celebrity parents sporting customized CDs include Patrick Dempsey, Brad Pitt and Angelina Jolie, Matt Damon, Debra Messing, Tori Spelling, Denise Richards, and many more.

Reality Check

The business is thriving now and going better than Candace and Eric ever expected. But the start-up costs were significant. Family was very supportive and Candace's dad is an accountant who shared his financial wisdom and backing for the new company.

With four performers and a full studio assembled to record the customized songs, **Name Your Tune** cost $25,000 to become functional in the very beginning. Candace and Eric also have West Coast partners that manage and grow the business in the States. They see it as a four-way partnership and each person has a specific job that makes the engine run.

Candace warns other aspiring entrepreneurs to protect themselves legally early on and to seek out expert advice from a lawyer. She and Eric sought out the counsel of many specialists to provide skills they did not possess. Defining their unique brand in the marketplace has been incredibly important as well as the research required to figure out the nuance of supply and demand in the kids' music industry.

At the end of the day, Candace is happy as a WAHM but warns other moms to be realistic about what you can commit to while raising your family. "Sometimes you have to learn to live with the fact that the beds aren't made and there are dirty dishes in the sink because you are working and growing your business while raising your kids. And that's okay!" Candace is still figuring out the delicate balancing act and no two days are alike. She wants her daughter to know that there is more to life than work even though as a WAHM she is never off duty.

Play it Forward

A portion of the company proceeds are donated to *Hear Here*, the nonprofit, charitable organization that purchases hearing aids for children through the Hospital for Sick Children. In 2007, Candace also launched a campaign called *Play it Forward*, a new initiative to support the Canadian Music Therapy Trust Fund. This effort collects new and pre-loved CDs to be distributed across Canada in support of Music Therapy. With the support and generosity of her customers, friends and colleagues, over twenty thousand CDs were collected and distributed last year.

The accolades keep rolling in since **Name Your Tune** CDs have been named as an iParenting Award winner, the Parent to Parent Award, and in 2010, both the CD was nominated for a Nickelodeon Parent Pick Award and Candace herself was nominated for an RBC Entrepreneur Award.

Out of a great idea, a song or two, and a lot of hard work and enthusiasm, Candace Alper changed her tune and reinvented her career from retail management-in-waiting to record label entrepreneur.

Candace's Advice and Action Steps:

- To the WAHMs – don't underestimate how hard it is to work at home.

- Empower yourself with information and seek help from others who do what you can't.
- Don't take things personally, business is business.
- Research the market you want to enter and find out what the needs are. Plan your transition according to what you love and what is needed.

Resources:

Name Your Tune: www.nameyourtune.com

66 It's only a good idea if you do it – so do it fully! 99

– Candace Alper

ભ ભ ભ ભ

35. LARA GALLOWAY: BE PROUD TO MAKE YOUR FAMILY THE #1 PRIORITY

As a self-proclaimed, fiercely independent, ambitious, and very satisfied IBM executive, Lara Galloway experienced a values shift that led to a new career. Living the life of a successful, double income, no-kids couple, Lara never envisioned herself with children. She had all the accoutrements of a corporate position plus the freedom to travel and lead a jet set existence – then life changed. She began to consider what she wanted her life to look like at age 50, 60 and beyond. It was then that she and her husband made the choice to have kids and she says, "…it was the best thing that ever happened to me."

Prioritizing What You Value

Lara now knows from experience how hard it is to create harmony in a mother's life. She also knows that moms often sacrifice their own needs and desires for the sake of their children, putting their own lives on hold for the future. So this mom-on-a-mission dedicated a new chapter in her career life to helping mom entrepreneurs earn more money doing what they love, while taking care of their number one priority – their families!

She became a certified life coach and combined her business acumen with her new coaching skills to create a community and a tremendous resource for women. Dedicated to helping others succeed, Lara knows that she is not alone as a mom entrepreneur. She tapped into a powerful and growing network of women and created her business: **MomBizCoach.**

When I spoke to Lara, her energy and enthusiasm were infectious. She is truly passionate about supporting moms who choose to be in business as a lifestyle choice. Now a successful blogger and radio show host, Lara's network has a wide-reaching territory including Canada, where she currently lives with her husband and three children.

Clarify Goals and Create Harmony

Her coaching and consulting services are geared toward creating harmony for moms who also want to be successful in their business. Lara helps her clients clarify goals, develop a plan of action, and she provides them with accountability and support. She customizes a personal development strategy that plays to each client's strengths, attitudes, and habits to work towards personalized success.

Lara's coaching approach is comprehensive and includes:

- Taking your business idea from concept to reality
- Personal branding, marketing, and networking
- Making the most of Social Media resources
- Creating a wealth plan and budgeting for it
- Teaching you to "get out of your own way" and sell yourself
- Setting fees and accepting them

Lara tapped into her transferable skills and knew the importance of relying on her former career experiences to propel her forward in her new business venture. One of the best things she learned from her days at IBM was customer service. She understood the value of returning calls and emails in a timely manner, and how to set (and meet or exceed) customer expectations.

Just Figure it Out!

Secondly, Lara learned that she can learn how to do just about anything. The start of her career at IBM was working in Public Relations; she then moved into Education and Training in a consulting role; and finally she wound up in executive-level sales and project management doing e-business for the automotive industry. She admits to knowing nothing about any part of that last role before she got the promotion, but within a few months was amazed at the new techno-language she was speaking and the e-commerce concepts she now understood.

> "So I don't get hung up anymore on not knowing how to do something. I just go figure it out by doing it. I apply this skill almost daily in my role as mom, entrepreneur, business coach, life coach, and marketing mentor to my clients."

But what about the steps that lie between launching a business and achieving success and financial stability? Lara is entering her seventh year of coaching. When she first started out as a coach, she was all about coaching and had no real interest in, or knowledge of, how to run a business. She struggled to find new clients, coached only one or two clients at a time and made hardly any money, which was mostly fine since she didn't define her goals around making money. It was clear to her that she needed the stimulation, challenge, connections with inspiring people, and the opportunity to "shine her light" and share her gifts more than she needed the money. Her work fulfilled her ambition, passion, talents, purpose, and was an outlet for her creativity that she needed to balance her role as a mom. Then, Lara had an epiphany:

> "About a year and a half ago, I made some big changes and got serious about running a business. I realized, to my surprise, that I was an entrepreneur, and I started studying everything I could about entrepreneurship, small businesses, marketing, being a *solopreneur*, etc.. I created my new brand/identity as the **MomBizCoach**, targeting a narrower niche of mom entrepreneurs. This focus has completely changed my ability to attract clients (rather than me having to go out and find them like I did before), and as a result, I've made more this year

in six months than I did in the last three years put together. I have an automated sales/marketing process that keeps my pipeline full of clients and is causing me to consider alternative methods of delivering what I do so that I can manage all the people who are ready to work with me. It's so awesome!!!"

You Can Have It All…Once You Know What You Want

In retrospect, knowing then what she knows now, Lara would have worked with a business coach to figure out her niche, her ideal clients, and how to craft her services as solutions to her clients' problems. Lara shared:

"…I wasted three solid years trying to explain to people what coaching is, and then tried to sell them coaching. I had no real understanding of how I was pushing myself, my thoughts, and my great ideas onto other people. It was a sales model that just didn't work. I wish someone had told me back in 2005 how to focus on my clients. I also wasted a lot of time not setting the proper boundaries around my work time, my family time, and me. I felt guilty about wanting to work and therefore only fit work in when nobody else needed me (i.e. when the kids were napping, sleeping, watching TV, playing outside, etc.). I also built up a lot of resentment because I wasn't making my needs and wants a priority, so I blamed my husband and my kids (mostly only in my mind) for my unhappiness back then."

Starting a new career is a journey and Lara's experience shows us some common growing pains and pitfalls. In time, she figured it out and is now thriving in her own business and able to help other moms with entrepreneurial aspirations. For those who think you can't have it all – a great career plus the opportunity to prioritize your family – you have never met Lara Galloway. Explore the possibilities with this mom entrepreneur and design your customized world!

Lara's Advice and Action Steps:

• Notice your definition of success – does it fit you? Create your own definition of success and work toward achieving that unique reality.

- Check in regularly with a coach or mentor who can keep you grounded and give you honest and supportive feedback and inspiration.
- Whatever you believe is true, so choose what you believe carefully. No matter what, believe in yourself!
- Be clear that this is your life and you are in control.
- Find a job you love and you'll never work a day in your life.

Resources:

MomBizCoach: www.mombizcoach.com
Five minute coaching MOMents on video:
 www.youtube.com/mombizcoach
Talk Radio: www.blogtalkradio.com/MomBizCoach
Savor the Success: www.savorthesuccess.com

66Whatever women do they must do twice as well as men to be thought half as good. Luckily, this is not difficult.99

– Charlotte Whitton

ℰ ℰ ℰ ℰ

36. TAKE A STEP FORWARD

Motherhood is a calling and I have tremendous respect for all the moms who work at home, at an off-site workplace, or as stay home moms. Being a mom is the toughest profession in the world and comes with unique challenges in the career world that are very different for mothers than for fathers. I have coached many new moms who have faced discrimination from employers when trying to re-enter the workforce because they chose to take extended time off to raise their children. For one of my clients, even a six-month work leave was met with the question, "How can you explain your employment gap?" from a prospective employer.

Working moms have the power to change that culture and negative mindset by taking their time away without guilt and re-entering the workplace with confidence and a sense of purpose when they are ready. It's a tall order indeed, but we must stick together and support each other since as women, we are all in this together. It's imperative to find organizations that will support your family-raising values. Here are some terrific resources to get you started:

- National Organization for Women: www.now.org/issues/ wfw/
- Fortune Magazine Report: Best Companies to Work for Women: www.money.cnn.com/magazines/fortune/bestcompanies/women/
- Working Mother www.workingmother.com

Vianesa Vargas, Pam Beattie, Candace Alper, and Lara Galloway are all WAHMs, the trendy new term for work-at-home moms. They have dedicated their lives to their families and their jobs and working from the home creates distinctive trials for them every day. But they have chosen this path because it gives them the freedom and the flexibility to call their own shots and prioritize things accordingly on a given day.

Invest in Yourself

Vianesa and Lara have created careers to serve as resources for mothers. By providing coaching, products, and other services, they are on a mission to help other mothers dealing with the realities of raising a family and growing a career. I strongly encourage you to find a career coach that can provide you with valuable insight, objectivity and resources to help you set and achieve your career goals. You need a plan, and a professional can help you formulate one that speaks to what you really want.

You would not build a house without blueprints, so don't underestimate what it takes to plan and build your career. Consider that coaching is an investment in your future, whether you are an entry-level professional or a seasoned, senior level executive.

Resources in Your Community

There are many additional resources available so check out your community to see what appeals to you. Adult continuing education classes at community colleges and local universities are great resources if you need to ramp up your skills in the workplace. The SCORE organization – counselors to America's small business (www.score.org) – has chapters across the country and targeted resources for women. Their services are free. The Chamber of Commerce in your respective city has networking events and training classes available that may suit your needs.

Look to your alma mater to see if they have alumni career coaching services available and a networking list serve or mentor pairing. Career coaches are a wise investment since they can be the conduit for all these resources and help you develop a plan that suits you uniquely.

The Joys of a Home Office

Pam and Candace are enjoying the proximity of their home offices. Working from home can be financially beneficial since you can write-off a portion of your utilities and office expenses on your taxes if eligible. See an accountant for the specifics. This can be a wise money-saving option as opposed to renting office space and incurring additional overhead costs.

Your home office may save you valuable commute time and enable you to multitask while working effectively on your professional tasks. I can just envision Candace cooking a batch of homemade spaghetti sauce between completing **Name Your Tune** work tasks. Sometimes the home office gives you the variety and flexibility that will make you happier at work. Others need the stimulation of coworkers to be content. As you are envisioning your reignited career future, think about your ideal work environment and consider whether the home office is a good fit for you.

REINVENTION TOOLBOX

Earning Versus Getting; Employing Effective Communication

The work-at-home moms, or WAHMs, have the difficult task of always being "on" in their 24/7 work/life environment. They have *earned* my respect and admiration for their intense work ethic and ability to multitask.

Let's take a look at "earning versus getting." One of my pet peeves is the client or student of mine who talks about *getting* their degree from a particular university or college. This nomenclature is everywhere from professional bios to all forms of the media. The last time I checked, schools were not giving out degrees to just anyone. Degrees are earned with hard work, diligence, and years of effort.

I encourage you to rearrange your mental furniture when it comes to earning versus getting in the professional world as well. You are in control of how people perceive you in the workplace or job search arena based on your professional behavior. Change your mindset and be clear about the accomplishments you have earned. Become the professional who can talk about your successes with humble confidence, and inspire others with your ability to self-promote in an appealing way.

Own Your Accolades

This technique of telling your story will come in very handy at a job interview or performance evaluation and it can be extremely helpful when you are making a proposal or enticing a new client to utilize your services. After all, you want to hear about how a business is successful before you buy their product or hire their services.

As customers, we expect references, referrals, and professional bragging about relevant successes before we buy into a pitch or a sale. We can learn the same lessons as individuals in the job-search arena or as experienced professionals looking to move up in an organization. It's time to own your accomplishments and help others understand how you achieved your successes. Telling these authentic stories helps others see your transferable skills and competencies and gives you credibility in the world-of-work.

Take credit for what you have earned and project your humble confidence. You work very hard to accomplish great things, so own these accolades!

Add "earn" to your vocabulary!

Practice (in the privacy of your home) talking out loud about your accomplishments so that you can prepare for networking opportunities and interviews. If you develop your success story and have it at-the-ready, you will be comfortable sharing it with others when the time comes.

Communication 101

I had the great pleasure of hearing Kathleen Oliver, COO of Oliver Winery (www.oliverwinery.com), speak at a professional development workshop. In her position at the winery, Kathleen manages the retail operation of the business, oversees the activities of the tasting room, special events, and human resources, so she communicates with a very large staff daily.

Kathleen offered these five tips for effective communication that I believe are universal to us all.

1. **Get to the point.** Communicating your point effectively and efficiently is essential in a professional setting. In a business where time is money, getting to the point can make or break a deal. Be sure to stay on track and avoid tangents and rambling. Stay focused, and relay your message with clarity and confidence.

2. **Get to know others.** With a large staff it's easy to lose faces in the crowd and not address people by name.

Make a point to get to know people within your department and beyond in your organization. Try to address people personally and learn about others so you can have meaningful interactions. Develop a system to remember names. Kathleen places photos of her employees on a bulletin board in her office, providing a means of matching names to faces, so that she can call each employee by name.

3. **Get along.** Follow the *Golden Rule* and treat others as you wish to be treated. It's that simple and applies to everybody at all levels within an organization.

4. **Get off the computer and get on the phone.** In this technology driven era it's easy to rely on email as the only way to communicate. Especially in a client-driven business, pick up the phone and make a personal connection. You may remember the old AT&T slogan "Reach out and touch someone." It's important to make that call when you can, and whenever possible, an in-person meeting is best.

5. **Get out of the office.** Be involved in your community and become an ambassador for your organization. Kathleen encourages her staff to volunteer and build their personal and professional relationships beyond the workplace. It's good for the individuals and ultimately, it's good for the company.

8

CONNECT WITH WISE WOMEN

Age knows no boundary in career reinvention. From twenty-something to eighty-something, the women in this chapter will inspire you with transitions that empower and engage. These ladies are playing to their strengths at every age.

37. ALMA BOND: FORGET EVERYTHING YOU LEARNED ABOUT RETIREMENT

Dr. Alma Bond had a 5th Avenue Manhattan psychoanalysis practice that she enjoyed for 37 years before she became a full-time writer at age 68. Her career transition came as result of a tragedy that inspired her to pursue the one thing she had not made time in her life to do – write full-time.

A very serious car accident, in which she almost lost her life, left Alma in a coma with seven broken bones and a concussion. Her recovery was slow but sure, and Alma knew that with a new lease on life she would pursue her passion and become a full-time writer.

Alma moved to Key West so that she could be anonymous and write, which was also a part of her recovery process. While Alma thought of Key West as the most creative place on earth, she missed her beloved Manhattan where she had led a writing group and gave presentations about her books. She decided to return to The Big Apple and pursue her writing there.

Power Point, Blogging, and Marketing for this Golden Girl

Now living in a Manhattan retirement home, Alma is enjoying what she describes as some of the best years of her life. In her 80s she is thriving and has had no fewer than 16 books published. *Margaret Mahler, a Biography of the Psychoanalyst*, was recently published by McFarland Publications and awarded a Finalist in the Biography category of the National Best Books 2008 awards, sponsored by USA Book News, and Finalist Book of the Year 2008 by Foreword Magazine. Her book, *The Autobiography of Maria Callas, A Novel* was First Runner-Up in the Hemingway Days First Novel Contest. Alma's most recent book, *Michelle Obama: A Biography* is currently in production with Greenwood Press and should be released early next year. Her latest manuscript, *Jackie O: On the Couch*, is presently with her agent.

When we spoke on the phone, Alma was busy preparing a Power Point presentation for her next speaking engagement. She maintains her personal website and knows how to market herself and her books. In fact, she responded to my HARO press inquiry for my book and blog project!

Alma developed a career as a successful writer on her own, securing agents and publishers through grit and determination. Her writing abilities were evident early in her life, and Alma recounted that at the age of 11 she composed a poem entitled "Ambition"; as she matured, her ambitions shifted from those of writer to those of psychoanalyst. As such, she had over 20 scholarly articles published in prestigious psychoanalytical journals.

Find out What's in Your DNA

Her scholarly writing certainly provided technique and a foundation for her biographies and novels. Alma says that writing is in her DNA and the only thing that gets her tired is not writing. While writer's block has never been an issue, Alma does miss the financial gain of a thriving psychoanalysis practice. The books are a labor of love, but they do not generate the same kind of income. Her goal is to hit the best seller list and earn a Pulitzer Prize some day, and I have every confidence that she will do so.

Alma is a woman who thrives on intellectual challenge and stimulation. She belongs to the International Psychoanalytic Association, the American Psychological Association, and is a fellow and former faculty member of the Institute for Psychoanalytic Training and Research. She also is a member of the Dramatists Guild, American Society of Journalists and Authors, Florida Freelance Writers Association, and the Writers Guild.

All in the Family

Alma also has a gifted and prestigious family, all of whom have published books. She is the widow of the late stage, screen, and TV actor, Rudy Bond, who appeared in, among other productions, the original Broadway production and the films *A Streetcar Named Desire* and *The Godfather*. His book, *I Rode a Streetcar Named Desire*, was published posthumously.

Alma is the mother of Zane Bond, Jonathan Bond, and Janet Bond Brill. Jonathan's book, *Under the Radar,* was published last year by John Wiley and Sons. Zane's book, *A Prophet Operating at a Loss*, was published several years ago by Writers Club Press. Janet's book *Cholesterol Down* was published recently by Random House and is a best seller.

Alma Bond is an inspiration for women considering a career change. Her advice: "Find what you love and do it!" rings true for all of us.

> "I can't stop. I get up in the morning, sit down at the computer and I am reluctant to break away even to meet friends. It doesn't take discipline to write, it takes discipline to stop writing. It is like having a love affair."

Dr. Alma Bond is evidence that life is what you make of it and that retirement is overrated. As an opera singer, I am eager to read Alma's book, *The Autobiography of Maria Callas: A Novel*, the story of the famous American-born Greek soprano. You can find Alma's books in retail stores and on Amazon.com.

Alma's Advice and Action Steps:

- Write every day and the word flow will come.
- Trust yourself and be your own best advocate.
- Anything you love is therapeutic – find what you love.

References:

Alma's personal website: www.alma_bond.tripod.com/
HARO – Help A Reporter Out: www.helpareporter.com/

> **"**Do it, do it, do it and enjoy a whole new life!**"**
>
> – Dr. Alma Bond

ભ ભ ભ ભ

38. Beverly Solomon: Object d'Art Model to Marketing Maven

Beverly Solomon began her career as a model and earned her way through the executive ranks of the cosmetics and fashion industry. At the peak of her career she made the decision to use her techniques in sales and marketing to promote the art of her husband, renowned artist, Pablo Solomon. Operating out of their historic ranch in the Texas Hill Country, Beverly was not sure that she could thrive without the action of the corporate fashion world but this wife/husband business is flourishing and proves that change can be good.

When I spoke to Beverly by phone we connected like longtime girlfriends who never missed a beat, even though it was the first time we'd met. She has a mellifluous Texan lilt to her voice that completes the package of this sophisticated and elegant professional woman. I was entranced by her career story that began at age 16 when she was drawn to the cosmetics counters in the Houston department stores.

How Fan Mail Turned into a Career Opportunity

Beverly grew up at the Estée Lauder counter and was mentored by the grand dames of the industry who showed her the ropes. But Beverly knew there was more than just the makeup counter in store for her career-wise, and she boldly sent a fan mail letter to Diane Von Furstenberg admiring her new fashion line. To her surprise, she received a telegram from Von Furstenberg asking for a meeting at an elegant Houston hotel. Needless to say, Beverly was star struck, but was also offered a job covering the entire Houston territory, modeling at trunk shows, setting up marketing and sales, and serving as a makeup artist. This was a pivotal time for the Von Furstenberg line with the launch of the now legendary *Tatiana* fragrance and the classic wrap dress that inspired Beverly's fan mail letter. This is the stuff that movie scripts are made of and Beverly was enchanted with her new opportunity.

After two years at Von Furstenberg, Beverly moved to a position with Revlon, which she calls the boot camp of the industry. This is where she developed her business acumen in sales and marketing. She worked incredibly hard and developed key relationships with professionals in the business and eventually moved on to a position with Ralph Lauren. She felt privileged to be a top level executive at a time when other women were just entering the workforce. Life was close to perfect before the recession hit and the fashion and cosmetic world changed. On a personal level, Beverly's life was also in turmoil. Her father passed away suddenly which affected her greatly. It was time to reassess and take stock of what was really important.

Working at Home with Your Husband

Longtime city dwellers, Beverly and Pablo came upon an 1856 historic ranch for sale in the Texas Hill Country north of Austin that would begin their life transition. They bought this beautiful property which became their home, Pablo's art studio, and also the new work space for Beverly, who is now serving as Pablo's Business Manager in addition to his full-time Muse.

What better way to capitalize on her skills in sales and marketing than to promote her husband's art? An ever-savvy businesswoman,

Beverly never lost her friends in the industry and frequently took trips to Houston and Dallas to be seen, in addition to promoting Pablo and his work.

But it was when a photographer friend took Beverly and Pablo under her wing that their art business developed a brand that made the difference in their bottom line. Pablo embraced a new Halston-inspired look with the requisite black sweater and jeans and Beverly was able to market his new personal image as well as the pieces he produced.

Ever the relationship builder, Beverly was able to connect with a fabulous network of art collectors, and from that network, cultivated clientele for Pablo's work. In these tough economic times, selling art is indeed a challenge. But Beverly has learned how to listen to her clients' needs and knows that selling a piece of art takes time and determination.

Don't Give In To the "Devil Boys"

Working with her husband comes with its own unique set of challenges, admits Beverly. They have set boundaries within the house – "He has his work space and I have mine." – so their work and life partnership can remain harmonious.

Beverly is incredibly planful and detail oriented, with a vision of the future that she has depicted in story boards and portfolios. Her goal, in addition to growing Pablo's art-buying clientele, is to develop and market art for homes and businesses. She talks about the *movie in her mind* that helps her visualize how she wants her life to play out.

> "It's easy to give in to the *devil boys* – the voices that tell you when you can't do something but I never want to live my life with regrets. I don't want to look back and say – I never did that. It's worth reaching out of your comfort zone to achieve your goals."

While the economy is not ideal for discretionary purchases, such as art, Beverly and Pablo remain positive and are enjoying the journey of their business together. With the rise of social media, Beverly has embraced technology as a way of promoting Pablo and his art. She is developing a data base to track customers and prospective clients since relationship building and stewardship is the bread and butter of the business.

Beverly has indeed made Pablo a recognized international artist who has been featured in books, magazines, newspapers, TV, radio and even a film. This elegant lady has forged a new career utilizing her skills and experiences from the fashion and cosmetics arena. She sums it up perfectly in her quote: "Don't fear beauty." And so, Beverly Solomon's career reinvention is indeed a beautiful thing.

Beverly's Advice and Action Steps:

- Never stop working on your dream and always be prepared.
- Use a storyboard or portfolio to illustrate your dreams and to give yourself focus and goals.
- If you work at home, set boundaries so that you can establish your own space and your own time.

References:

Beverly's personal website: www.beverlysolomon.com
Pablo's personal website: www.pablosolomon.com
HARO, Help a Reporter Out: www.helpareporterout.com

> **"**When my life looked like it was falling apart, it was actually falling into place.**"**
>
> – Beverly Solomon

ॐ ॐ ॐ ॐ

39. Karen Kibler: Earning a PhD at Forty-Something

Karen Kibler was raised in a small farming community in Iowa and what many people don't know about her is that she can weld and operate heavy equipment. She earned her Bachelor's degree from the University of Iowa in 1977, and soon after relocated to Arizona and worked several jobs in the business sector from receptionist to business owner. At age 40, she began working on a PhD which she minted in 1997 from Arizona State University where she now serves as an Assistant Research Professor and the university Biosafety Manager. The focus of her current research is HIV vaccines and treatments.

A Turning Point at Age 40

When Karen turned 40 she found herself in an accounting job with a very low pay ceiling and no room for advancement due to her lack of a business degree. Her undergraduate degree was in science, so she decided to pursue work in that field. After applying for a few positions, she got incredulous responses because it had been 15 years since she graduated, with no science-related work since then. Because science had always been a passion, she decided to apply for the graduate program in Microbiology at Arizona State University. Much to her surprise, she was accepted and left her accounting job in January of 1993 to start grad school – one month before her 41st birthday.

Karen was a nontraditional student starting a PhD in her forties, but her maturity, passion, and discipline served her well. She developed a strong interest in working on HIV and set her sights for a post-doc position at the National Institutes of Health in Bethesda, Maryland, and landed a very competitive position in one of the NIH research labs.

The Rewards of an Authentic Career Fit

After two post-doc positions, Karen took a faculty position at her alma mater, ASU, where she taught classes in addition to working on her lab projects: development of an HIV vaccine and novel HIV treatments. As a Research Scientist, she works on the cutting edge of new treatments for HIV and admits that it takes a lot of patience and perseverance to make advances in research that will solve health problems.

A research project can take years to yield any results, so Karen acknowledged that her current work values are different than those of being an accountant – not better, just different. As a biosafety professional charged with helping researchers maintain compliance with regulatory requirements, she has been part of a team that helps prevent lab accidents, and finds that very rewarding.

Channel Your Energy

Pursuing a PhD in her forties was challenging for many reasons. Re-acclimating to the academic regimen was tricky enough for an older student, but mustering the energy to deal with the round-the-clock schedule was indeed a trial. Karen now counsels young people who want to pursue graduate degrees to do so as soon as they finish an undergraduate program so that they can capitalize on the momentum.

For Karen, in the life sciences, earning a PhD involved about 20 hours of teaching per week, 10 to 15 hours in class and then all the rest of her time to study and pursue research. Financially, graduate school was challenging, too. With the intense research, teaching, and study requirements there was no way to have an outside job; and the academic stipends were not enough to make a living wage. Karen graduated with significant educational debts, but she saw the degree as an investment in her career future.

The career landscape in the life sciences has changed dramatically in recent years. With fewer tenure-track university faculty positions, many PhDs leave academia for the private sector biotech/pharmaceutical companies or for government positions. Others pursue law or MD programs, but career scientists have to think broadly about how they want to apply their skills after they earn a PhD.

Change is Constant

One thing that Karen has learned in her lifetime is that you can always depend on things to change. When making the decision to reinvent herself and transition careers, Karen was determined and focused which helped her remain confident in her decision. She also did her homework and went into the PhD program with her eyes open. While she didn't know exactly what jobs she would pursue after the degree, she knew the additional credentialing would empower her to break through the proverbial glass ceiling.

Karen has also experienced dramatic change on a personal level many times in her life. After an emotionally devastating divorce, she experienced clinical depression. Years later, Karen found the book *The Cracker Factory*, a wonderful resource to better comprehend the healing and self-understanding required of those who suffer from depression. Five years after reading the book, her second husband was killed in an accident and Karen fell into another round of depression which inspired the book she wrote, *The Second Chasm* (Wyatt-MacKenzie Publishing), which was published in January of 2009.

Karen's book is unique because it bridges two of the most common losses faced in the world: divorce and widowhood. Her stories of recovery offer a message of hope as she describes the journey from despair to healing. Not only did the book prove to be an emotional catharsis for Karen, it launched her freelance proofreading career as well. One would expect detail orientation from a scientist and Karen fits the bill working as a proofreader/editor consultant with Wyatt-MacKenzie Publishing.

It's clear that Karen has found a place of peace in her life and is pursuing a career with many facets that she enjoys. She encourages others considering a transition to do their due diligence and reflect upon what is meaningful for them. This research scientist hopes to bring a resolution to the work she has been doing on an HIV vaccine. She also plans to continue pursuing her work as an author and editor. There are several books floating around in her head which Karen aims to write down some day. Indeed, it took courage to pursue a PhD in her forties and Karen Kibler is now thriving!

Advice and Action Steps:

- Do your homework and research new career options to find your best match.
- Don't be afraid to go back to school as an adult – it can be exhilarating.

- Embrace change.
- Don't give in to negativity – focus on the positive. Don't waste energy on self-doubt. You must believe in yourself.
- Pay attention to the special moments.

Resources:

The Second Chasm Book: www.thesecondchasm.com
Wyatt-MacKenzie Publishing: www.wymacpublishing.com/

66 Remember that love and friendship are gifts we give,
with no requirement that they be earned. 99

–Karen's mantra

ॐ ॐ ॐ ॐ

40. SUSAN VERNICEK: IDENTITY CHECK

A twenty-something, native New Jersey girl, Susan Vernicek put her Fine Arts degree with a dual focus in Graphic Design and Photography to use working in the graphics department of a medical company. While she enjoyed that job, she still had a percolating entrepreneurial spirit within her that needed to be released. The two driving forces in her life from a young age have been to run her own business and to have a positive influence on others. The end result of sticking with that focus and owning her passion was the creation of **S&J Identity, Inc.** – a unique and empowering online magazine created to help women accept, appreciate, and achieve.

> "Being a woman with many interests, and all the same concerns as my female counterparts, I relied on the media for information that could help improve and inspire my life. Through my own discontentment with all the in-your-face ads and useless information about diet fads, fashion trends, and celebrity gossip found in other magazines – *Identity* was born.

I believe our role models should be in our everyday lives; not photo-touched fashion plates on a page. *Identity* is my gift to every woman, for being who she is, and the best that she can be."

Day to Day and Breath by Breath

Susan is indeed an enlightened young woman, ahead of her time in many ways, who already understands the female mind is often full of doubts, questions, and insecurities. Her magazine is a positive resource and a safe place to turn for information, sharing, and permission to just be who we are. *Identity* is not a fad site with quick-fix diet tips and fashion fads or beauty cream miracles. It celebrates real women with everyday issues by providing practical resources. Susan's mission is to encourage readers to embrace their inner confidence and to achieve their potential without comparing themselves, their ideas, and their bodies to others. Targeted at the 21 and older demographic, *Identity* features articles by guest writers who share their expertise on a variety of timely topics.

Working "day by day and breath by breath" (Susan's mantra), she says her goal is to make *Identity* her full time occupation so that she can leave her day job altogether. In this tough economy she finds it scary to leave the financial security of her graphics position, but also understands the struggle and the need to move forward so that *Identity* can have her full attention and time.

Susan recognizes the freedom of being her own boss at *Identity* and can play to her strengths and her passions by helping women with her online publication. She believes we have a responsibility to pay-it-forward to younger women and help them understand their gifts and the ability to embrace their self-confidence early. Her ultimate goal is to reverse the pervasive negativity trend and help women think more positively about themselves.

With an artistic background it's easy to see how Susan uses her graphic design skills for *Identity*, but she admits that without a business background she looked to mentors and established resources to help her launch the magazine. Her dad and brother both own businesses and proved to be terrific resources for her new venture. An avid researcher, Susan also did her homework and asked a million questions to learn the best practices for online magazines. As a New Jersey resident, she also tapped into a Garden State resource designed to help young entrepreneurs – New Jersey Young Entrepreneurs.

The challenge continues to be balancing the day job with the growing demands of the magazine. Her financial strategy is to pay for new things as she can and increase incrementally. The goal is to continue to reach all 50 states and grow her sponsors and advertisers.

Just Do it Already!

The main framework of *Identity* was designed by ImpressM, LLC, but with Susan's expertise and knowledge of HTML she can manage most of the site herself and provide graphics for clients who need it. She reports that although she seeks out some contributors, many actually come to her. A future goal is for Susan to work with universities to develop workshops for women featuring the expert contributors from *Identity*. She is planning a Friday morning radio show to go along with her Identity FACT Friday!™ on the site and eventually, a book!

Susan has a go-for-it attitude that has helped her achieve success with *Identity*. Starting with no expectations and an open mind she was determined not to hold back and to stay true to herself during the entire process. Always eager to learn new things and to set new goals, Susan has learned to trust her instincts and push the envelope to grow her business.

> "I am strong, positive, and extremely ambitious and these qualities have gotten me where I am today. My advice is to JUST DO IT ALREADY! Pick a starting point and go. Then give yourself homework each day. Ask yourself a question then find the answer and move on to the next. There isn't always positive feedback, support, or an answer, but you have to work around that. Get rid of the negative in your life. You can't move forward if you associate yourself with negative vibes. I know it's easier said than done, but you CAN do anything you put your mind to. Take it day by day, breath by breath. Accept. Appreciate. Achieve™"

Words of wisdom from an insightful young woman on a mission to help us celebrate our unique identities.

Susan's Advice and Action Steps:

- Set goals so that you have benchmarks for achievement; give your-self homework every day.
- Embrace the strengths you have and use them.
- You have to be willing to take the plunge if you are unhappy in your current career. If you never try something new, you won't ignite your passion.
- Find your circle of trust (family, friends, mentors) and bounce ideas off them to flesh out your mental plans.

She has also trademarked these phrases for *Identity*:
- Feel Beautiful Everyday!™
- Accept. Appreciate. Achieve.™

Resources:

Identity: www.identitymagazine.net
National Association of Women Business Owners NAWBO:
  www.nawbo.org/
Ladies Who Launch: www.ladieswholaunch.com/
Savor the Success: www.savorthesuccess.com
New Jersey Young Entrepreneurs: www.njye.webnode.com/

"Day by day, breath by breath."

– Susan's mantra!

ひ ひ ひ ひ

41. TAKE A STEP FORWARD

The women in this chapter show us that reigniting or reinventing a career is an ageless endeavor. From Susan in her 20s to Alma in her 80s and Beverly and Karen in between, it's never too late or too early to find a new calling.

Create Vision Board

As you will discover in the Chapter 8 *Reinvention Toolbox*, a portfolio is a powerful tool that can be used to showcase your skills and experiences to a new employer or during a promotion review. But before you interview for the dream job, you must come up with a vision that illustrates your future goals.

Magazines, websites, and newspapers are overflowing with stories and images of people, items, places, and experiences that just might ignite your passion. Clip stories and photos that motivate you and save them in a vision folder that you can look through for inspiration. If you respond to visual stimuli, use your favorite images to create a vision board to make a collage of the images that motivate you. The concept is to surround yourself with motivational descriptions of what you want. When you become inspired to act, then you will be more likely to find those people, places, careers and experiences in your real life.

Beverly Solomon used this technique very successfully when transitioning into her new career. It created the visualization she needed to move forward with her plan. Based on the law of attraction, design the vision you want to live. You can use the low tech version with a cut-out collage on a cardboard base and place it prominently in your living and/or work space. Or, you can opt for an online tool that helps you create a vision board with your favorite music, images, and animation layouts with Orange Peel Systems: www.visualizeyourgoals.com.

Put Your Passion to Work

You've heard over and over from many different women in this book to identify your passion and put it to work. I'm thrilled that so many women have articulated this same theme since they were not prompted by me, don't know each other, and represent a diverse group of individuals from a variety of backgrounds and careers. The one thing they do have in common is career reinvention and the fact that they are now in careers they thoroughly enjoy. This should help you understand the importance of finding your passion.

Identifying your passion is one thing but **the goal is to monetize it and make it part of your career path.** It may surprise you that some of the most successful people are the most passionate. They find ways to incorporate their personal passions into their day-to-day work. Start by integrating your passions into your current career and see if this leads to new opportunities that maximize the ability to use your passions.

For example:

- Passionate golfers take clients to the golf course and talk about business on the links. Many successful deals have been closed during a golf game.
- People who are passionate about photography never leave home without their camera. They take photos at work events and publish the images on the company website or newsletter whenever appropriate.
- Creative or imaginative people express their innovation regularly. They are constantly trying new approaches to old problems and finding clever solutions to daily tasks.
- Professionals who love to socialize attend networking events and make regular plans to have lunch with friends or colleagues.
- People who enjoy public speaking join organizations like Kiwanis, Rotary, and others, to take advantage of opportunities to address public groups on their favorite topics.

By taking baby steps and incorporating your passions into your current career, you will find ways to rejuvenate an existing position or, you can develop a new opportunity by playing to your passions more regularly.

Be Proactive and Recharge Your Career

People who incorporate passion into their career don't just fall into this situation. They very deliberately incorporate their passion into their jobs. If you like to write, volunteer to author content for the company website, newsletter, or intranet. If you are energized by people and enjoy travel, volunteer to attend every conference you can as a representative of your organization in the industry. The magic happens when your boss and your colleagues see you in your element, thriving and playing to your passions. When you demonstrate success in what you like to do best, your managers will be more likely to find additional ways to let you shine.

Hang out with passionate people who share your passions. Find the other artists, sports fans, writers, gardeners, theatre lovers, etc., and network with them just as you would in your career life. These passion connectors can lead to new career opportunities as well as newfound friends who share your interests.

Be curious and read a book or magazine about a topic you know nothing about. Wander the web and find sites and blogs that you never knew existed. Talk to people that you don't already know and learn something new as often as you can. New passions can arise in the most surprising places and when you find something that lights your fire, you just might consider this as a new career endeavor.

Retooling for a Change

Sometimes a career reinvention involves a new opportunity that is beyond your current skill set and experience. It's never too late to re-credential yourself, and Karen Kibler showed us this by earning a PhD in her forties. Whether earning a degree or pursuing workshop certifications to enable you to be eligible for new career opportunities, these additional credentials can often be the ticket to position eligibility.

Research wisely before you jump into a degree program. During a recession, graduate and professional school applications spike since people often find a safe harbor in an academic program when jobs are scarce. Investigate the field you are pursuing to learn if the degree you seek will enable you to find a job in that particular career sector. Just because you earn an MBA doesn't entitle you to a job in the business sector. You still need to be a full package candidate who can articulate why you are a value-add for an organization. The degree doesn't automatically mean you will find a job.

Finding your bliss, putting passion into your work life, and being proactive will help you gain career satisfaction. Passion is a career asset and if you read the biographies of people you admire you will often see how they integrate passion into their lives. If you need to add skills or credentials to your professional toolbox, first consider what you are working towards and make sure it corresponds with your goals. Career reinvention is timeless. I've had multiple career reinventions and I fully expect to have many more!

REINVENTION TOOLBOX

Use a Portfolio as Your Secret Weapon; Embrace Change

Fine artists have been using portfolios for decades to showcase examples of their work. This multidimensional tool is gaining popularity in the job market for other professions as well. By assembling an archive of your work, you can show employers why you will be a value-add to their organization.

Similar to the resume, the portfolio should be customized for each unique opportunity. You should include your resume and/or CV as well as letters of recommendation, quotes, or special comments from key constituents and examples of what you do well that is relevant to the new job opportunity. A mission statement can articulate why you want the job as well as why you are an excellent match for the position.

I like to include a list of my top skills with descriptions of how they will be applicable to the new job. A goals or future plans section can help you articulate how you will grow in a particular role in the organization. Employers will see you as a strong, long-term investment for their team.

If writing is a desired skill for the new job, include samples that showcase your best work and a variety of styles. Get creative and use graphics or photos for visual pop but keep text pithy and succinct using bullet points and tag phrases instead of long paragraphs.

Leave a Lasting Impression

I encourage my clients to bring the portfolio to the interview; walk your future boss through the document and leave it behind after the interview, which allows the hiring committee to have a lasting impression of you as a candidate.

Spiral-bind your portfolio so that the pages are secure, and be sure your full name and contact information appear clearly on the cover page. While you want to show the breadth and depth of your experience, keep the portfolio brief so that the readers don't lose interest while viewing.

This secret weapon can set you apart from the competition. An added bonus of assembling a portfolio is the valuable self-reflection process that will put you in tip-top shape for your interview, giving you the opportunity to focus on your strengths in an articulate manner.

Can you Handle Change?

A transferable skill that tops the list of competencies which employers value most is the ability to handle change. While change is an essential element in life and career, most of us instinctively resist it. The ability to handle change requires ongoing attention and perseverance. In the career arena, learning to deal with change can be used to your best advantage.

Keeping an open mind when change is imminent in your place of work will help the powers-that-be to recognize that you are a true team player. When you look to grow, rather than focus on the possible negatives of change, the process becomes easier. If you adopt a negative attitude about change then your energy is wasted on this behavior, and your productivity decreases as well as your professional worth within the organization.

If you are in a position of authority in your organization or pursuing an entrepreneurial venture, be sure to motivate your team and help them through the growing pains of change. By rewarding success, you will create internal champions from among those who are higher risk takers and more aware of the value of new outcomes. Be enthusiastic and persistent with your team to help them re-boot the negative hard wiring that is often the first response to change.

The Power of Being a Change Agent

I know that sometimes change comes unmercifully with lay-offs and downsizing. I encourage you to let your feelings out and experience the full gamut of emotions since it's a vital part of catharsis and moving forward. When you resist your emotions you simply make them stronger. I have established a 24-hour pout period when I allow myself to rant and rave in the privacy of my own home about a disappointment – then I move forward and focus on what I can control.

I have seen many people make lemonade from the career lemons they have been dealt in this tumultuous economy. Believe in yourself and know that life is what you make it because **change is constant.**

- Write down the major changes you have handled with grace during the past year.
- Utilize these stories as part of your interview repertoire when pursuing a new job or pitching a proposal. The ability to handle change is a powerful asset.

9

EVERYTHING HAS ITS PLACE: HOW TO FIND YOURS

The women in this chapter have capitalized on former career experiences to move forward with new opportunities. In this day and age, people change careers an average of five to seven times during their adult lives. I believe everything happens for a reason and with these women everything also had a time and a place.

42. KARI DIFABIO: SAY "CHEERS"... TO A NEW CAREER

Kari DiFabio had tears of joy in her eyes when she earned her Elementary Education degree and couldn't wait to get started on her career as a teacher. After teaching multiple grades in Arizona and Nevada she had a revelation that launched her personal career change. "Sitting in the teacher's lounge one day, my life flashed before my eyes and I saw myself 20 years down the road, unhappy and bitter if I stayed in this career." Following her intuition, Kari quit teaching, moved to California, and lived with her grandmother while she figured out what to do next.

A Transitional "Fun Job" That Turned Into a Career

As a way to generate income while she figured out her next career move, Kari took a part-time job at a winery in a small tasting room, earning just pennies above minimum wage.

"After I left teaching, I found the wine business by asking myself, 'If I have to get a job while I figure out what I want to do with my life, what menial job sounds like the most fun?' I believe I found something I enjoyed because I took the pressure off myself to find the *right* job."

Kari learned a lot in her first job in the winery tasting room by asking many questions and absorbing information from her coworkers. It was like learning a new language in the beginning and visiting other vineyards expanded her industry acumen. While some family and friends thought she had jumped off the solid career bridge, Kari remained positive and enjoyed her new work experience in the winery. She loved the blend of science and art, intellect and creativity, and even though this was not a long-term job, Kari discovered it was a starting point and had tremendous growth potential. She moved on to sell wine to key accounts as a distributor in Los Angeles for several years.

"I realized early after I left teaching how many skills I had that I considered transferable. As a teacher, I was managing a team of 20-40 people (albeit "little" people) and had daily tasks that included sales, communications, PR (parents), staff management, and teaching. I decided I was just as equipped for the business world as anyone. So, during my first wine sales interview, the manager interviewed me. He was an old-timer of the business and looked it, kind of like an old cowboy who could eat you up and spit you out at breakfast. He looked over my resume and said almost with a sneer, 'So you were a teacher. What makes you think you can sell wine?' I looked at him and replied without blinking, 'I sold algebra to eight-year-olds. Do you really think selling wine is going to be hard for me?' I got the job."

As with any new career transition, Kari faced a lot of challenges. It was financially difficult since her first sales job was 100 percent commission in the lowest-producing territory and the thought of not being able to pay the rent was terrifying to her. Her grandmother always served as a mentor and inspiration and she encouraged Kari to persevere and ignore the naysayers.

The Power of Self-reflection

As she progressed through different jobs in the wine industry, Kari moved to Napa and pursued a thoughtful self-reflection of her values, interests, personality, and skills to find a more meaningful position that was a good fit for her in the industry. She considered what a dream day would look like at work and started a list that included: working for someone she respected, working in a beautiful environment, being allowed to use all of her talents and abilities in one position, not being micromanaged, and having an opportunity to work from home.

On a whim, she logged onto a Wine Jobs website and found her current position at Sodaro Estate Winery. Her employer shared, "We knew immediately that Kari was the right fit for the position." The rest is history.

Although Kari has autonomy over her entire work day, self-motivation is essential. "The good part is that you are all by yourself, the bad part is also that you are all by yourself!" Sometimes she misses having an office environment to bounce ideas around and although the winery staff works independently, they are definitely a team.

With the world of social networking, Kari is learning to become adept at utilizing Twitter and Facebook to keep Sodaro Estate's wine in the limelight of a competitive industry. You have to be a Jill-of-all-trades in a smaller company. She's now a tech person, a marketing person, a sales person, a hospitality person, a VP business person, an accounting department, and an office manager all-in-one. Way to multitask, Kari – although she does have a part-time assistant who helps greatly.

Dare to Design Your Dream Job

She got all the dream job wishes on her list and now works from home as well as at the beautiful Sodaro Winery – a breathtaking landscape that reflects the stunning beauty and individuality of this estate. Working with renowned winemakers Bill and Dawnine Dyer and Don Sodaro, Kari is thrilled to have colleagues she respects.

Kari sees life as a continual journey and hopes to own her own business someday. For now, she is thrilled to hone her skills and work in this dream job at Sodaro Estate Winery, and is thankful she had the courage to admit that teaching was not a good fit. It's liberating to know that we can change our career minds as often as we wish and this teaches us all to trust our gut instincts. Cheers to Kari on her self-assessment and reinvention!

Kari's Advice and Action Steps:

- Follow your intuition no matter how quietly it speaks; follow what calls to you – no matter how crazy it sounds.
- Get specific about what you want – make a list and make it happen.
- Test drive different jobs/ideas until you find what suits you best.
- Make excellent mistakes – that is how you learn, and life is a journey.

Resources:

Sodaro Estate Winery: www.sodarowines.com
Savor the Success: www.savorthesuccess.com

66 Don't ask yourself what the world needs, ask yourself what makes you come alive and go do that. Because what this world needs are people who have come alive. 99

– Harry Thurman

43. DEBBIE WAITKUS: HOLE IN ONE

Always an athlete, Debbie Waitkus played on the soccer team at the University of Arizona; after graduate school she went on to establish a thriving corporate career as president of a 37-year-old, 130 million-dollar private mortgage banking firm. She always attributed golf as one of her keys to success since she would take her clients on golf outings to establish and steward professional relationships and business deals. When the CEO of her firm implemented a new strategy that didn't follow suit with her professional values, Debbie knew it was time for a change and what better way to plan her reinvention than to leverage the game of golf in a new business.

The Power of a Personal Coach

Debbie utilized the expert resources of a personal and executive coach, Silver Rose, whom she first encountered when she brought in Silver as a consultant on a project while she was still working at the firm. Debbie hired Silver personally and began exploring an exit strategy and new options for her career future.

Her professional reinvention began with weekly one-on-one calls with Silver and detailed homework assignments on self-assessment and personal tracking. She conducted informational interviews with business peers and joined a mastermind group that works as an advisory board of sorts to provide motivation and accountability – all under the tutelage of her coach. Debbie also joined Toastmasters and a few networking groups for outreach, education, and personal growth purposes.

Silver gave Debbie permission to explore, and she realized that golf – her passion – was also an educational tool and a business opportunity ripe for developing. Her knowledge about how to generate business through golf empowered Debbie as a resource others wanted to learn from. She also saw a tremendous opportunity to build confidence in businesswomen through strategies incorporating golf.

Move Over Boys – Women Are Playing Golf, Too!

According to Debbie:

"It's a known fact that women, as a group, don't participate in the game of golf to the extent that men do. For the most part, they see the game of golf as a mystery to which only men hold the key. Yet, the message businesswomen hear today is that golf is a widely accepted playing field for conducting business and they are missing out on opportunities by not participating. The golf community has created women-only golf clinics targeting the female executive. Statistically, women are the largest new group coming to the game of golf today. Yet, often frustrated with their skill-set, they are also the largest group that leaves the game and does not return."

So Debbie capitalized on demystifying this critical business skill that can be used successfully on the golf course. Her business, **Golf for Cause™**, teaches women (and men) how to use golf as a business tool, to create opportunities, and to forward relationships because it's more than just about going out and hitting golf balls. **Golf for Cause™** provides the keys and the tools to demystify the game.

In her new role, Debbie enjoys being 100 percent responsible for the success and failure of each strategic decision in her company. She has control over her schedule; her work product matches her integrity and is a more accurate and rewarding reflection of who she is and what she wants out of a career. Debbie also appreciates the opportunity to set a positive example for her children by doing something that makes a difference and by giving back to her community.

Making Money Playing Golf

While the new career sounds too good to be true, Debbie has learned a lot over the years. Her initial business plan was not realistic and included programming that does not fit her business model today. The plan required some tweaking and adjusting over time. With a small staff of only two (including Debbie) she doesn't have a large team to rely on as she did back at the firm. Debbie has learned that she can only control so much and that delegation is not always an option. A perfectionist by nature, Debbie also learned that delivering the perfect program was unrealistic. "At some point you need to step up to the ball and hit it off the tee!"

Since golf is now her livelihood, another important lesson learned was to identify which programs work well and which generate meaningful revenue. The economy has also been a challenge and the meeting and events industry has taken a particularly hard hit. Many companies have cut training and professional development budgets entirely. Debbie learned quickly that she needed to stay flexible and open to new ideas and partnerships in order to grow her business.

A personal goal for Debbie was to keep her schedule free enough to travel with her daughter, a student athlete, to national tournaments and college recruiting trips. This was a liberty she gave herself with the new business that would not have been possible at the firm. She also set up administrative systems to enable the business to run smoothly in her absence.

> "I set up systems such that I have an assistant who works remotely and maintains my database, follows up on various tasks as needed, brings forward ideas, keeps me on task, etc. Finding the right person was an incredible challenge as I spent a lot of time and money getting systems in place and then checking, redoing, and re-educating. With the right person in place – I'm free to work 'on' the business and not 'in' the business."

Mission Accomplished

The mission of **Golf for Cause™** as an organization is to develop and deliver products and services that move others to use golf as a dynamic strategy to achieve their objectives, focusing primarily on business professionals new to the game, especially women.

While Debbie benefited from the expert counsel of her coach, Silver Rose, she also suggests that women seeking a career change develop a support network to help stay properly focused on goals and to provide a level of accountability.

She suggests that new entrepreneurs work with a good accountant from the start to better understand which strategies are effective and meaningful tax-wise for the business.

Birdies and Bogeys Lead to Great Business

Debbie's repertoire of golf educational opportunities provides a myriad of topics such as:

- The secrets even successful business owners and managers don't know
- Create an even more rewarding business environment
- See how your business success and your golf game are a reflection of who you are
- How to improve both your business and your golf score

Participants usually spend half the day in the classroom using golf as a metaphor to learn what differentiates being an entrepreneur, manager, or technician, and how this applies to the business world. After the classroom session, participants hit the course and play nine holes of golf in a strategic format. All levels can participate, even never-played-before beginners. The day ends with a facilitated debriefing session, awards, and refreshments. An ideal group size is 6 to 40 participants, and Debbie customizes programs to fit an organization's or individual's needs.

The reviews are in and Debbie consistently scores big with her clients! The programs are experiential and golf anchors the learning. Debbie's repertoire of golf educational opportunities provides a myriad of topics such as:

Mental Mulligans: A fun and enlightening team-building workshop for your group that reveals how you present yourself both in and out of the office, on and off the golf course. Learn to understand different behavior styles on the golf course and how they impact your game and your success in business!

Get in the Game – Business Golf with On-Course Mentoring: A great way for business professionals to add golf to their business tool boxes.

Tee Off Program: A half-day outing designed to prepare the newer golfer (or non-golfer) who wants to make a positive impression when playing in a charity or industry golf tournament.

Nine and Wine: A golf mentoring program offering a casual golf experience, designed especially for new golfers (men and women) to help them feel at ease on the tees. Golf up to nine holes with a mentor, with a facilitated debriefing, networking, and hosted happy hour after golf ("wine" not "whine!").

Birdies, Bogeys and Business – Success On and Off the Course: a program that Debbie co-created and delivers with Joyce Friel from Peak Performance Consulting (www.peakperformancecorp.com). This half-day program uses golf as a metaphor to learn what differentiates being an entrepreneur, manager, and technician – and the implications for you and your business. Explore your ownership mentality and create an even more successful business environment.

By discovering new fairways and approach shots for defining business objectives, relationship development, and marketing strategies, Debbie Waitkus has turned golf into gold.

Debbie's Advice and Action Steps:

- For all the perfectionists – let go already and just do it!
- Consider a professional career coach and/or a resource team to assist you.
- Find a good accountant early on if you begin a new business.
- Really think about what you are passionate about doing – your next career may be right under your nose.

Resources:

Golf for Cause: www.golfforcause.com
Silver Rose, Coach: www.silverspeaks.com

66The bad news is time flies.
The good news is that you're the pilot.99

– Michael Althsuler

ↅ ↅ ↅ ↅ

44. ALICIA SABLE HUNT: FOOD EMPOWERMENT

Alicia Sable Hunt, known to all as Sable, grew up in the Hamptons in the 1980s during the height of materialism, big money, and a recreational drug culture that was rampant in this affluent east coast community. She benefitted from the very strong grounding of a religious household and ended up attending nursing school, an anomaly in her group of friends, most of whom pursued high-profile and high-paying corporate careers. Sable attributes her passion for helping people to her mother who instilled strong values in her at a young age.

A Nurse in the Kitchen

Always comfortable in her own skin when working with patients, Sable experienced a variety of settings in the medical field from bedside nursing to intensive care, and outpatient clinics. But she developed a love for oncology care working with cancer patients. With 15+ years under her belt as an oncology nurse, Sable understood the immense struggle of those fighting cancer and the nutritional challenges they uniquely face. Proper nutrition is paramount during cancer treatment but many patients suffer from loss of appetite and taste, preventing them from receiving the nourishment they need. Sable feels strongly that patients should be able to thrive while continuing with their daily lives during cancer treatment and recovery. Championing the cause in 2006, she stepped into her kitchen and began baking up a solution, and **Sable's Foods** was born.

Knowing that cancer patients needed food that met specific nutritional requirements as well as flavors and textures that would be appealing and easily digestible, Sable started experimenting in her kitchen. She also wanted something portable so that patients could maintain a sense of normalcy and an active lifestyle while in treatment. Sable developed the first iterations of a nutritional bar that was baked like a brownie and bursting with flavor and *nutritional empowerment* – Sable's slogan and branding platform.

The Proof is in the Pudding...or the Nutritional Bar

Sable introduced her bars to her patients to get constructive feedback and the ultimate taste test. They gave very helpful suggestions about flavor and content. For example, she discovered that consuming granola and whole nuts, like in a traditional health bar, caused digestive problems in her patients. She was on a quest to develop the balance of flavor, texture, and nutrition that would make her bars unique and beneficial for her patients.

It was time to call in the experts, and Sable consulted with nutritional and oncology specialists, as well as an executive chef and food product consultant, to develop the ultimate version of the bars that are now on the market. The bars are widely sought after by cancer patients and athletes, as well as others in search of nutritional empowerment.

The journey doesn't end with Sable's great tasting and nutritionally sound bars. She is dedicated to keeping the ultimate goal of curing cancer in sight. To that end, a portion of her profits from product sales are donated to nonprofit organizations actively pursuing solutions to cancer care issues, including prevention, diagnosis, treatment, and symptom management. In her words, "A *bite of every bar* is donated to cancer research."

A Labor of Love and Experience

It may sound like Sable just waltzed into her kitchen and created her empowerment bars overnight, channeling her inner Betty Crocker; but the reality is that it was a long and intense journey from conception to product development and eventually, sales. The business officially launched in 2009, as Sable worked 80+ hours a week as a consultant to pay the bills to allow her to bring **Sable's Foods** to life during the evening and weekend hours.

In addition to being a Registered Nurse, Sable also earned her MBA so that she would have a full understanding of the business world. She founded the **Edwards-Hunt Group, LLC**, to facilitate basic and clinical research by implementing contemporary solutions for today's translational medicine challenges. She provides multilevel consulting services to the nonprofit arena, commercial bio-repositories, and technology companies. This is a fabulous illustration of how she tapped into her transferable skills and maintained an active consulting practice while growing her new business. Sable admits that the empowerment bar business idea was a leap of faith. She is a linear thinker, a cerebral person, and she found it difficult to work with the artists and product consultant experts she sought out to develop her website, marketing materials, and company brand. But she believes that "Every time a door closes, a window opens." And she believes that **Sable's Foods** was meant to be.

Her Patients are the Inspiration

She advises others interested in starting a new business to "Write a business plan and let someone else challenge your assumptions." It's a brutal test, but an important part of building your brand and a viable product or service. Sable learned early in her journey to check her ego at the door, and believes that she tapped into her woman's sense of survival to make her business and consulting firm happen. She has no fear, and realized that if she doesn't work, she doesn't get paid.

Sable has a favorite mug that says: "What would you attempt to do if you knew you could not fail?" This has become a mantra and helped her forge ahead with unbridled energy and enthusiasm. Ultimately, Sable is still inspired by her patients and created **Sable's Foods** to help others. She is proud to nurture herself and her loved ones with her nutrition bars and is responding to increased patient demand to develop new flavors and additional products.

Sable's Advice and Action Steps:

- Have the guts and confidence to take a risk.
- Interview people in-the-know in your particular line of work and tap into their expertise.
- Define what you don't know and then find experts that do!

“Why not!”

– Sable's mantra

When faced with a new opportunity this mantra has served her well.

Resources:

Sable's Foods: www.sablesfoods.com
Savor the Success: www.savorthesuccess.com
Edwards Hunt Group, LLC: www.edwardshunt.com

ᘔ ᘔ ᘔ ᘔ

45. KIM DALY, THE URBANE CONCIERGE

Kim Daly has worn many hats during her professional career, from an Executive Briefing Program Manger to the Director of Global Travel Operations. In her previous life, Kim was working a full 40-hour week and spending 20 additional hours running errands and doing a plethora of other miscellaneous tasks. Her free time was hardly spent doing the things she wanted to do. She soon discovered that there were many people in the same position – their lives were lost to mundane chores.

So, Kim created **The Urbane Concierge** for people like her. But rather than simply start a personal assistant service, she wanted to offer something special. For 30+ years Kim worked as an event planner and global travel arranger, and her clients demanded a unique experience. And that's what she vowed her new company would offer. Kim's concierges are experts at delivering intangibles beyond simply serving your needs. They become an extension of yourself, anticipating your requirements and accomplishing tasks the way you would want them to be done. That's why all her services are customized and Kim wouldn't have it any other way. Many people start businesses out of necessity, and that is certainly the case with **The Urbane Concierge.** Kim was ready for a change.

Wanted: Chief of Staff for Your Life

The very definition of an urbane concierge is: affable, balanced, cosmopolitan, courteous, cultivated, gracious and mannerly. These days, hiring the equivalent of a "Chief of Staff" is more common than you think for everyone from business owners to corporate managers and stay-at-home moms. Yet, as our lives get more complicated, the role of personal assistant has grown in scope to include highly sensitive and confidential tasks such as project managing for small business owners, paying bills, managing the individual services for your home (i.e. gardening, housekeeping, remodeling), personal and business travel arrangements, even overseeing your social calendar. There are tremendous benefits to having someone within arm's reach who can juggle what you never have time to do.

Kim believes that in reality, work time is intermixed with personal time. Her clients need far more than a junior assistant: they need a trusted adviser, a concierge who is standing by 24/7. **The Urbane Concierge** provides customized packages so that clients can focus on their core competencies and strengths and leave what they don't enjoy doing in the capable hands of a concierge. In return, life is simplified and clients can have more balance to enjoy non-work time with friends and family.

I Can't Get No Satisfaction

Kim started her business after 30 years in the corporate sector because she was extremely unhappy in her professional life. She felt as if she was selling her soul to her employers and had to compromise her values to make a good living. In March of 2007, she quit her job and began to research what else was out there.

She knew her strengths: she enjoyed the organizational and detail-orientation skills that came naturally to her, and she also enjoyed helping others. But she wanted to utilize her skills on her own terms. Kim was a frequent conference attendee at the Professional Business Women of California (PBWC) events and became inspired to branch out on her own after attending a PBWC program that had an entrepreneurs track.

With the input of a SCORE (Counselors to America's Small Businesses) advisor, Kim quickly developed a business plan, a web design logo, and applied for a tax ID number. Soon after, she assembled an amazing team of women whom she knew and trusted from her professional contacts, and the business officially launched in October of 2007.

She chose the name **The Urbane Concierge** because she wanted to reflect the unique services offered that distinguished her from other personal assistant companies out there. Branding is especially important for a new business and Kim did a lot of self-reflection and research to consider what her special sauce would be in this service industry.

A Very Special Valley Girl

Demographic research was also very important when Kim approached the question of where to focus her business. She has captured a niche market in Silicon Valley and the San Francisco region. Ninety-five percent of her clients are men and ninety percent come from within the San Francisco area. These young professionals are very busy and career-focused, so they need **The Urbane Concierge** services to handle their multifaceted lives. This high-end clientele is the definition of urbane and they see having a personal concierge as a status symbol as well as a necessity, and that's good for business.

In her business, Kim often has access to a client's personal bills and medical records, etc., so discretion and confidentiality is of the utmost importance for her and her staff. Kim relies on having a stellar reputation as well as positive recommendations from clients. This is the number one way that her business grows.

The old adage – The customer is always right! – is alive and well. However, according to Kim, there are some clients that just can't be helped; she has learned that in some cases she must turn down a client if she thinks it won't be a good fit for her or her staff. This is the beauty of running your own shop – you can say no to business you don't want.

Über Organized

In some cases, Kim talks about working herself out of a job because she gets a client so organized that they don't need her anymore.

But that is usually a good thing because it results in a strong referral and the original client most often comes back for another service down the road.

While being organized is what Kim does best, she admits that some clients seem to have monumental tasks to accomplish. She trains her staff to keep their game faces on and to remember that "fear breeds courage" and to persevere at all costs. Since her team is made up 100 percent of contractors, she hand picks which concierges on her staff are best suited for particular assignments. Kim does the original client intake to build trust and determine how **The Urbane Concierge** can best help.

At the end of the day, Kim now values that she is completely accountable and responsible for the satisfaction of her clientele. She runs her business on integrity and trust and believes she is making a contribution in the lives of real people that she gets to know very well. Developing these strong professional relationships has given her a newfound satisfaction on the job and she enjoys being her own boss.

One-Stop Shop

The goal is to make the client aware that a concierge is a one-stop shop for all of their needs. Kim offers customized packages and pricing for each client based on what they require. A sampling of services includes, but is not limited to:

- Appointment setting
- Home life organizer
- Help Small Business Owners Manage Projects
- Travel and event planner
- Personal shopper
- Errand runner/courier
- Home greeter
- Pet care
- Project Manager

Your Wish is My Command

Kim has developed packages and customized services for individual and corporate clients, so the possibilities are endless depending on what a person needs. The first question in an intake is usually about cost. Why should they employ someone to do what they usually do for free? Kim has them fill out her *Urbane Concierge Time/Cost Assessment*, something she encourages clients to do before they even make an initial appointment. Suddenly, their mindset changes and they realize they actually need a concierge because Kim adeptly shows them that their time is valuable and time equals money.

Here is an example from one of Kim's customers. The client billed $300/hour as a business coach. She also estimated she spent 10 hours per week running errands, shopping, and so on. That is $3,000 per week at her billing rate, or $156,000 a year! After employing **The Urbane Concierge**, she not only saved money and time, but also found she had more energy to devote to both her business and her personal life.

Studies have shown that 75 percent of employees handle personal responsibilities while on the job. To make matters worse, 92 percent of employees admit to taking personal time off just to keep on top of their errands and personal responsibilities. Kim's business mission is to take care of people's needs so that they can focus on their core competencies and enjoy life more.

Time Flies

The business launch in October of 2007 seems like more than three years ago and Kim is thriving as a business owner. In 2009, she was named one of the Top 50 Women Entrepreneurs by Savor the Success. In 2010, Kim was awarded a full scholarship by Wells Fargo for the Fearless Entrepreneur Program. Future goals include continuing to build her clientele as well as her team of experienced concierges so that she can focus more on growing the business and handling select clients. She is conscious about staying on top of current trends, techniques, and technologies to better serve her clients.

Kim is now living her philosophy that time is money and she appreciates having control over her own time now. She has numerous client testimonials on her site that endorse **The Urbane Concierge** and validate that Kim's career reinvention was well worth it!

Kim's Advice and Action Steps:

- Find the right people when building your staff.
- Be tenacious for what you really want.
- Realize that some clients can't be helped and that is no reflection on you – simply move on.
- Use technology to your best advantage. Keep abreast of new gadgets, programs and features that can help you in your work and life.

Resources:

The Urbane Concierge: www.theurbaneconcierge.com
Savor the Success: www.savorthesuccess.com
Professional Business Women of California: www.pbwc.org/
SCORE: www.score.org/index.html
Wells Fargo Fearless Entrepreneur Program:
   www.futurewomenleaders.net/entrepreneurship-program

> ❝People have hired me because of me.❞
>
> – Kim Daly

ℱ ℱ ℱ ℱ

46. TAKE A STEP FORWARD

Learning to find your unique place in the career world can be a daunting task. The exploration process will help you learn what is out there so that you can find a new opportunity that aligns with your VIPS – values, interests, personality and skills. The women in this chapter all took a deep look inside themselves to discover what made them tick. Kari DiFabio and Debbie Waitkus utilized the informational interview process as a way to learn what the possibilities were for new careers.

Inquiring Minds Want to Know

The informational interview is a nonthreatening way to ask professionals in your industry of choice for advice, guidance and most importantly, for information about their career field. It's very difficult to learn about a job just by reading a position description. By talking with people in the field you can get the skinny about work tasks, company culture, salary and benefits, and many of the off-limits questions that are not appropriate to ask during an actual job interview.

Keep in mind that you always need to bring your professional best to an informational interview. Dress the part and behave like a future employee. These sessions can lead the interviewing professionals to inquire about your career future, which opens the door to discussing how they might be of assistance, or to what degree they are willing to make network referrals.

Don't forget to thank the people with whom you meet by sending a hand-written thank-you note. Keep in touch regularly, as needs change in an organization frequently. If you made a positive impression you may be the first on their list when a position becomes vacant that you are well suited to fill.

Lastly, ask your connections if there is anything you can do for them in return. Make the networking a two-way street and be willing to pay-it-forward and help when you are able.

Volunteer Your Way into a Job

By giving away your skills in the form of volunteerism you can showcase your value to others while doing a good deed. Get involved in your community and take on a leadership role. Amazing things can happen when people give of themselves to a worthy cause. They learn important skills and form powerful and positive relationships that often lead to future opportunities. Feeling good about the work you provide as a volunteer is energizing, and can be the motivation needed to get you into the public eye so that you are not a well-kept secret.

Scratching the Entrepreneurial Itch

Many of the women I interviewed moved from careers in an organization to an entrepreneurial venture. Sable Hunt, Debbie Waitkus, and Kim Daly in this chapter, started their own businesses to enjoy the freedom, flexibility and independence of being their own boss. They found a way to monetize their passion. But these ladies can attest to the fact that business owners have total accountability for the success and failure of every task they pursue. Great risk is required to create a successful new product or service and to develop a brand that is unique and desirable.

Keep in mind that you don't have to jump ship and head out to sea on your own to scratch the entrepreneurial itch. There are numerous opportunities inside existing organizations for exercising the industrial muscles you may have. Take a closer look inside before you make the jump outside to make sure that you have exhausted all the resources at your disposal in your current workplace. You might be surprised at the opportunities available down your own company hallway. Sometimes you just need to change roles in an organization to find career satisfaction. Consider having a confidential heart-to-heart with a Human Resources Manager whom you can trust to give you sound internal career advice in your organization.

When to Quit the Day Job

At present, nearly six out of ten people are actively seeking new positions or are considering starting their own company due to career dissatisfaction. My strongest bit of advice is not to leave a job until you have another position to go to. Besides the financial risk of not having a steady income, you are far more employable when you **are** employed than when you are looking for a new job without a current position.

I encourage the career-changing women I coach to ease incrementally from a job they don't like until they can secure a new position, or start to earn income with their new business venture. For example,

Sable Hunt has her consulting business to ensure financial security as **Sable's Foods** grows and becomes fiscally solvent. Others work part-time to be able to devote more time to career exploration or job interviews but still have some money coming in and a fresh reference from a current employer. Phasing out of one job and into another can often ease the stress of transition.

REINVENTION TOOLBOX

The Art of Self-promotion; Leadership Lessons; Play Nice in the Career Sandbox

It's not enough to just do your job well anymore. Professionals need to distinguish themselves in the workplace in order to earn promotions and recognition within an organization. Entrepreneurs have to take control of their own career advocacy to be noticed and stay competitive in the marketplace. The art of self-promotion is a necessity but walking the line between humble confidence and inflated ego can be difficult.

Here are some strategies to help you get more recognition on the job:

1) **Be a Social Butterfly** – Don't just work in isolation. You need to socialize with people, have emotional intelligence, and social awareness in your organization. Your visibility at work is just as important as your competency. Your positive attitude will take you places, and colleagues at all levels of the organization should be aware of what you are accomplishing for the company.

2) **Understand Company Culture** – It is very important that you understand the culture of your organization. It's all about how you fit in and assimilate into your career environment. You don't need to change who you are, but you should identify the potential to grow your career and mold yourself accordingly. Company culture ranges from fashion style and quitting time at the end of a work day to going above and be-

yond for a special project. Adapting to your firm's culture will empower you to be recognized as a team player.

3) **Develop an Expertise** – In addition to having a broad span of transferable skills, develop a niche skill that is unique in the company and you will quickly become the go-to person for this much-needed proficiency.

4) **Embrace Your Humble Confidence** – Nobody likes an egotistical bragger, but if you can learn to talk with humble confidence about the accomplishments you earned, you will quickly become an asset to your organization. It's necessary to be able to talk about what you do well in performance reviews so keep a record of what you have accomplished during a given time period and be ready to discuss this if your boss asks what you are doing, at any time.

4) **Be a Team Player** – You can rarely accomplish anything solo in an organization. Being a team player not only provides you a holistic picture about the task but also helps you broaden your skill set. Team work is an opportunity to be connected to people from other groups and divisions in your organization. This enhances your chances to move up in your company and increases your visibility throughout the organization.

5) **Network, Seek Feedback, and Have Mentors** – Build your personal Board of Directors at work and seek feedback and constructive criticism regularly. Don't wait for a performance review to ask for pointers; be pro-active and seek out mentors within and beyond your organization.

6) **Make an Impact** – The impact can be on the company's bottom line or significant work you do in the community. Be an influencer; give back or pay-it-forward to ramp up your visibility at work.

You are in the driver's seat when it comes to your career self-promotion. Learning to be your own best advocate will help you achieve your goals within an organization and beyond. It takes practice and a conscious mindset, but the art of self-promotion is doable for all.

Women Leaders

Former Secretary of State Madeleine Albright is paving the way for the future women leaders of the world and unlocking the door to the proverbial *good old boys' club.* At Wellesley College, Ms. Albright's alma mater, a new Institute for Global Affairs named after her will offer students around the world access to nonpartisan lectures, seminars, and internships, with topics ranging from political science and economics to religion. The goal is to address the issues at the core of international societies and empower women leaders with an opportunity to make a difference.

Albright believes that women see the human part of issues and pursue power in order to do something with it, not just to have power for the sake of having it. With only 600+ women holding cabinet positions worldwide, Albright is on a mission to groom the next generation of women leaders.

Here are some key competencies for leadership success:

- Good leaders should foster the potential of others in an organization.
- Optimistic leaders are more effective.
- Effective leaders learn to be assertive and not aggressive.
- Strong leaders are comfortable in their own skin and lead by being authentic and true to themselves.
- Successful leaders understand human motivation.
- Valuable leaders give their team the space to work autonomously.

Playing Nice in the Career Sandbox

I have learned that there is nothing stronger than the power of women in community and that women can be inspirational resources in the professional arena. But I also know the reality of being a woman in the professional world and how we often struggle with owning a strong, confident persona while maintaining our authenticity and honoring our femininity at work.

Learning to play nicely in the proverbial work sandbox does not have to be that difficult. Here are some strategies that will help you become a good team player but still empower you to stand out and make your mark on the job to earn the recognition you deserve.

- **Preparation equals credibility.** It's that simple: be prepared and you will earn the respect of your colleagues and impress the powers that be.

- **Pick your battles.** There will be difficult situations, but don't fall on your sword for every cause. Be mindful of your values and what is really important to you as well as what will empower you to advance in the organization to achieve your goals.

- **Own your confidence.** In order to succeed you must believe in yourself and your abilities. By tapping into your humble confidence you can project an image of self-reliance, poise, and assurance that will give your team faith that you can get the job done.

- **Be aware of your surroundings but focus on you.** On a team you must be cooperative, but at the end of the day, you have to be your own best advocate and be ready to take charge of your career future. Don't wait for a boss or supervisor to groom you for greater things; be proactive and strategize about ways to upgrade your standing in the organization.

- **Don't Gossip.** The old adage, "If you don't have anything nice to say, don't say anything at all," still rings true. Avoid hallway gossip and treat your colleagues with courtesy and respect. What goes around comes around and you should expect the same professional treatment from others.

- **Be aware of yourself and your values.** It always comes back to who you are, what you value, and how you want to show up in the world. Take stock of how you want to make your mark and align your personal and professional values so they are validated for you at work.

10

A CALL TO NURTURE

From nurturing house guests to abandoned farm animals, these women have turned taking care of others into a career.

47. JACQUELINE EDELBERG: HARNESSING THE GOODNESS OF HER NEIGHBORHOOD

An academic by training, Jacqueline Edelberg earned her PhD in Political Science and taught at the University of Osnabrück in Germany as a Fulbright scholar. After the international teaching stint, Jacqueline returned to her beloved Chicago with her husband, Andrew, ready to give birth to their first child. After a very complicated and difficult delivery, Jacqueline was relieved and fortunate to have a healthy baby. The experience ignited her maternal instincts and she wanted to focus completely on nurturing her infant daughter for the next six months.

While Jacqueline relished her new role as a mother, the pangs of career guilt began to set in for this professor-turned-mom who craved intellectual stimulation and challenge. Struggling with the proverbial question of "What do I want to be when I grow up?", Jacqueline took the advice of a dear relative who shared that raising a child is a special time in a mother's life, and a very short one at that. She cautioned Jacqueline to enjoy this time with her daughter and to be confident that the work would always be there when she was ready to go back. Little did Jacqueline know that her future career would be to mobilize a grass roots movement rehabilitating neighborhood schools in her Chicago community and across the nation.

Mother Knows Best

Jacqueline took this wisdom to heart and started to believe that her skills would not go away and that her role as a mom was very important. In addition to her training as a professor, Jacqueline is also a fine artist, a painter who specializes in ketubahs: distinctive Jewish marriage agreements which have become a significant form of Jewish ceremonial art. Painting was something she continued to enjoy while pursuing the full-time career of being a mother.

From the time her daughter was an infant, Jacqueline's husband Andrew agreed to pursue the research about where their daughter would attend school. However, Chicago parents, like parents across the country, face the same sobering reality: given the scarcity of spots, it's extremely difficult to get your child into an expensive private school. Entry into a respected public magnet school isn't any easier. In fact, Jacqueline points out that it's statistically easier to get your high school kid into Harvard than to get your kindergartener into a selective enrollment magnet school. In Chicago, most middle-class parents believe that their non-selective neighborhood public school is *not* a viable option.

Most parents assemble portfolios with glossy brochures and consultant recommendations to figure out where to send their kids to kindergarten and beyond. Andrew passed the baton to Jacqueline and the school research became her responsibility. Finding a suitable school for her daughter, Maya (and son Zack, who was on the way), was a top priority.

The Power of the Roscoe Park Eight

Struck with the possibility of moving out of Boystown, her fabulous Chicago neighborhood known for its architectural charm, rich culture, diversity, and tolerance, Jacqueline convinced her friend Nicole to come with her to check out Nettelhorst, her neighborhood's underutilized and struggling public elementary school. After a 3-hour tour of the 110-year-old building, the new principal, Susan Kurland, asked what it would take for them to enroll their children. Stunned by her candor, they returned the next day armed with an extensive wish list. Susan read their list and said "Well, let's get started, girls! It's going to be a busy year…"

And so the journey from Roscoe Park to the school began. Jacqueline and Nicole recruited six more park friends to join the cause. The women called themselves the Roscoe Park Eight, and met once a week in a Boystown diner, to plan how to fix Nettelhorst so their kids could walk to school.

Eight Women in a Diner

This meeting of the minds may have started humbly in a diner, but never underestimate the power of mothers on a mission. The talent pool within the mommy brigade was deep, ranging from lawyers and advertizing executives to artists and bankers. They decided to call their group, The Nettelhorst Parents' Co-op, with the motto "We do more during nap-time then most people do all day!"

The Roscoe Park Eight set an ambitious goal: the Parents' Co-op had just nine months to reinvigorate Nettelhorst. These women were scrappy, creative and spirited, and as Jacqueline admits, too naïve and green to know how difficult this endeavor really was.

Running on infectious energy, each park mom captained a Co-op team: infrastructure, public relations, marketing, special events, fundraising and curricula. Each woman was assigned a task that best met her skill set and experience, and each team had to succeed concurrently. The team captains then set out to recruit as many families as they could to join their fledgling cause.

Mommy Moxie

How could the Co-op refurbish a school with a budget of nothing? The moms began cold calling people to solicit services, supplies, and volunteers with skills and an interest in the project. In the beginning, fundraising efforts were futile since nobody wanted to contribute to a failing city school. The development team was disbanded and efforts were refocused on getting the necessary goods and services donated for the cause.

In a matter of months, the community donated over half a million dollars in goods and services, contributed inch-by-inch and a gallon of paint at a time. The beauty of this project was that anything you had to offer for the cause was perfect. If you had a gallon of neon yellow paint, great! Nothing was turned down and nothing was wasted. The community joined in, and now there isn't an inch of the school that hasn't been touched by a neighborhood artist. The whole school is an inspiration!

The community buy-in was extraordinary and people started calling from distant parts of the city to contribute to the reinvention of Nettelhorst. The Roscoe Park Eight truly harnessed the goodness of a neighborhood. The story has been featured on *Oprah & Friends*, *NPR*, *CNN*, *60 Minutes*, *Education Weekly*, and in the local Chicago media.

Sustaining the Cause

Eight years into the project of fixing Nettelhorst, Jacqueline wrote a book about her experience: *How to Walk to School: Blueprint for a Neighborhood School Renaissance* (Foreword by Arne Duncan and Afterword by Rahm Emanuel). The book chronicles the highs and lows of motivated neighborhood parents galvanizing and then organizing an entire community to take a leap of faith to transform a challenged urban school. They successfully turned Nettelhorst into one of Chicago's best schools, virtually overnight. Jacqueline proved that the fate of public education is not beyond our control. In the book, she provides an accessible and honest blueprint for reclaiming the great public schools our children deserve.

The original eight moms wanted to create a sustainable school that could thrive into the future, and now, Nettelhorst is one of the most desirable schools in Chicago. Enrollment has doubled; test scores have tripled; and parent involvement is off the charts. The teachers and administrators are also thriving and proud to be part of the school's renaissance.

The original fundraising committee may have been unsuccessful at first, but now that the school is thriving, development efforts are a well-oiled machine. For example, parents forged a deep, mutually beneficial partnership with the Stanley Cup-winning Chicago Blackhawks. With a $210,000 donation, the Blackhawks built a state-of-the-art fitness center in the school and an outdoor hockey field. Players, coaches, and team managers frequent the school, teaching kids about sportsmanship, discipline, and maintaining healthy lifestyles.

Thanks to the work of driven parents, the school now has the financial wherewithal to maintain the building, and to provide innovative programming to enhance an already solid curriculum.

Labor of Love

While the moms contributed sweat equity to this cause eight years ago, and did all the work pro bono, Jacqueline is still on a mission to continue with the renaissance of neighborhood schools nationwide. America is based on the neighborhood school model, and that model succeeded in this country for over a century. Jacqueline is obsessed with sparking the national grass roots movement since so many of America's neighborhood schools are now in sad shape. According to Jacqueline, "If everyone just fixed their own neighborhood school, we could see real, systemic change across the country."

Jacqueline has led workshops for the Community Schools Initiative, Northside Parents Network, and Chicago Public Schools on how public schools and reformers can stimulate communities to improve public education. She has consulted with schools and neighborhood groups on issues of strategy and organizational development. Her goal is to insert this idea into the national dialogue about education.

The story is inspiring on so many levels, but in addition to reinventing a school that was literally falling apart at the seams, Jacqueline reinvented herself in the process and established a brand new career. Harnessing her transferable skills from the academic and artistic arena, this mom has a passion for changing neighborhood schools across the country, so that kids can walk to school in their own communities.

Take Back the Schools

The next step for Jacqueline is to generate a steady income as a change agent consultant for neighborhood school reform. As the story of Nettelhorst spreads, she's gaining momentum on a national level. If you have an interest in reforming your neighborhood school, be sure to contact Jacqueline. *How to Walk to School* provides a blueprint that any community can duplicate – with a little elbow grease and a lot of passion.

While doing a good deed that would enable her own children to walk to school, Jacqueline unearthed an accidental career that has inspired her to continue this work in other communities. Her success proves that good things do happen, often when you least expect them.

Jacqueline's Action Steps for Reforming Your Neighborhood School:

1. Form a group of core parents.
2. Find a Principal you can work with.
3. Find a pro-bono lawyer.
4. Get the school spruced up.
5. Start a public relations program.
6. Enroll your own kids in the school.
7. Get the community involved in the school.
8. Settle in for three or more years of open houses and fundraisers, volunteering at the school, and meetings out the wazoo.
9. Acknowledge you're not going to get any breaks.

Resources:

How to Walk to School the Book & Blog: www.howtowalktoschool.com/
Nettelhorst School Video: www.youtube.com/watch?v=XPZr6BYJSGc

> "Never doubt that a group of small thoughtful citizens can change the world. Indeed, it's the only thing that ever has."
>
> – Margaret Mead

❧ ❧ ❧ ❧

48. Anne Shroeder: From the Embassy to the Farm

Anne Shroeder has been through many transitions in her life but at age 50 she has now found her passion and peace with a dream career that will warm your heart. She splits her time between her web-development business, **Language Works,** and caring for 50+ animals in need of a home. Her animal sanctuary, **Star Gazing Farm,** is a nonprofit organization and if that wasn't enough, Anne is also refining her skills as a sheepshearer.

She Bought the Farm!

As a graduate student, Anne studied Linguistics and specialized in Arabic which led her to an interesting, but according to her, "dead-end" job at the Saudi Embassy in Washington, DC, where she worked for five years. Willing to retool in order to make a living, Anne enrolled in a vocational computer programming school and taught ESL (English as a Second Language) on the side in addition to waitressing to make ends meet. She took a course on the Internet and fell in love with web development where she still works as a freelance consultant, developing sites for small businesses, nonprofit, and government clients. She also teaches web design at the local community college and has a flexible schedule which permits her to fit in her other passion – animals.

Anne first moved to the suburbs from the metropolitan life of Washington, DC, so that she could adopt a dog. In 2002 she bought a farm in Maryland after experiencing the realities of this lifestyle when she served as a "farm sitter" for a friend who has a 150-acre farm in Virginia. She found it invigorating to work on the farm and with the animals and turned her farm into a nonprofit she named **Star Gazing Farm** where she takes in abused, stray, and unwanted animals in need and provides them with a permanent home.

Tending To Her Flock

Anne believes that farm animals are every bit as affectionate, interesting, and in need of loving care as other domestic animals and there is a real need in her community for more compassionate farm animal care. With 50+ animal residents on her farm, including a small flock of sheep, Anne discovered that it was very difficult to find sheepshearers so she went to sheepshearing school and now adds this to her list of transferable skills.

Word leaked out that Anne has become a fine sheepshearer and she travels to other farms in Maryland, Virginia, West Virginia, and Pennsylvania to shear small flocks. She has since learned to shear Angora goats, llamas, and alpacas and has turned this into a thriving little business to supplement the farm operational expenses.

Pay-it-Forward

As a nonprofit organization, **Star Gazing Farm** has an education and outreach division. Every year they teach children and young adults about the humane care of farm animals and help them build physical and moral strength through actual hands-on farm work. In 2007 they began a program tailored to local at-risk youth.

With Anne's sheep shearing skills, she offers experiential classes and demonstrations with wool and fiber, showing participants how to shear, wash, card, and spin the wool they grow. The local community is made up largely of urban and suburban residents and Anne has invited them in to visit and to volunteer to befriend the sanctuary animal residents and develop a greater compassion for farm animals.

Between sheepshearing and website design, it's still difficult to make ends meet on the farm with the high cost of food, veterinary care, and appropriate housing for the animals. So Anne offers opportunities for animal sponsorship, contributions, and volunteer work to make **Star Gazing Farms** run efficiently. Since Anne can't take in every stray or abandoned animal, she also runs a farm sanctuary network through her website to help find permanent homes in other locations for animals in need.

The Challenges of Running a 501c3 Organization

While Anne believes that she graduated from the school of hard knocks and admits to being very stubborn and determined, in the beginning she found herself out of her element trying to care for her many different farm animals. She bought books on farm animal caretaking and joined discussion lists online about caring for ducks and sheep and quickly became familiar with the local veterinarians.

The future goal is to have a larger corps of volunteers for her nonprofit that can assist the Board of Directors with fundraising and development for the organization. Anne believes there are many private donors who would support **Star Gazing Farm** if they knew it existed; her goal is to be financially solvent so that she can continue to develop additional education and outreach programs.

By day Anne tends to her sheep, goats, birds, dogs, cats, horses, cows and pigs – 50 in total. At night she works on her web-development business, and often stays up past 2:00 a.m., well aware that she has to be up at dawn to tend to the animals. Admittedly, she has the biorhythm of a "Web Vampire" and is able to keep these taxing hours because she is doing what she loves.

Follow Your Heart

While work/life balance is often impossible, Anne is doing what she loves and shared that she has found her calling. After many career changes it's refreshing to hear Anne talk about her work with such passion and enthusiasm. Working in the Saudi Embassy as a Linguist, I'm sure Anne never envisioned being the Founder and Director of a nonprofit, a freelance web developer and a sheepshearer. It pays to follow your heart. Check out the **Star Gazing Farm** website and consider sponsoring one of Anne's animal residents today. Their full bios and histories are posted on the site and your generosity will be much appreciated by the likes of Newman the goat and his friends.

Anne's Advice and Action Steps:

- Don't be afraid to explore new careers but do your research, pursue informational interviews and inform yourself.
- Follow your heart.
- Have a vision.

Resources:

Language Works: www.language-works.com
Star Gazing Farm: www.stargazingfarm.org

> **"Attitude is more important than the past, than
> education, than money, than circumstances, than
> what people do or say. It is more important
> than appearance, giftedness or skill."**
>
> – W.C. Fields

ఈ ఈ ఈ ఈ

49. KAREN VANDERGRIFT: A FIXER-UPPER PROPERTY IN URUGUAY

Soon after college, Karen Vandergrift began a glamorous career in the hotel industry working 14-hour days and rubbing elbows with celebrities. Yet, she had a creative muscle that was not being massaged and yearned for balance in her life since she was burning out in a big way at a very young age. She left the hospitality industry in 1990 with no intention of ever returning. Never, say never....

From Horsehair to an Inn of One's Own

Karen went back to school and earned an MFA in textile design and opened her own company selling custom horsehair fabrics. The venture was successful but a financial failure, according to Karen, so she set it aside and traveled with her husband. They discovered Uruguay and fell in love with the country that had a decidedly European feel. Sixty-five percent of the residents are of Italian descent and Karen says you feel as if you are in Tuscany. She thought this would be a wonderful place to produce her textiles.

In 2002 she and her husband bought a derelict property there that needed a lot of work to even be considered habitable. Karen had the ability to visualize the potential in the property and began to discover the hidden architectural jewel that had fallen into disrepair. So began the labor of love to restore the 1830s house and outbuildings perched on a bluff overlooking a gorgeous river and 80 acres. This was to be the site where she would entertain family and friends. In the beginning, she didn't even consider marrying her strengths and interests in entertaining, promotion, catering, design, and launching a new career with the rebirth of a luxury Inn at Estancia Tierra Santa.

Overcoming Language Barriers, Social Anxiety and Not Fitting In

This project was not without major challenges before the Inn was ready for public consumption. Needless to say, Karen was in Uruguay where everyone spoke Spanish. She quickly learned to get by with enough Spanish to be able to communicate with local vendors and relied heavily on the internet for things she could not access in her new community. This was quite a cultural shift for a woman who hailed from San Francisco!

A self-proclaimed introvert, Karen had to overcome some social anxiety and put herself out there to earn the trust of the locals who were critical of her renovation project. She also experienced a major shock in this male-driven "macho" society that was not accustomed to a woman launching her own business. While she claims she is still earning their respect, Karen took the time to get to know the locals and gained their trust as a fellow business owner. In 2007 Karen opened the Inn doors to her first guests with a satisfaction beyond her wildest dreams.

"I had several distinct advantages, including considerable luck and good timing, in the purchase and renovation/construction of the property. In 2002, when we purchased Estancia Tierra Santa, the Uruguayan economy was suffering because of its close ties to the Argentine economy which had collapsed in 2001. Wealthy landowners in Uruguay are mostly Argentines who look to Uruguay as a secure investment. The owner of the estancia at that time was an Argentine yacht broker, whose business had collapsed and was therefore seeking to liquidate some of his assets, including Estancia Tierra Santa. He was desperate to sell quickly and we made a low-ball offer which he immediately accepted."

Luck Meets Preparation

Labor costs were quite low in Uruguay then, again owing to the economy, so Karen immediately began employing laborers to clear the land and clean up the main house and outbuildings. Wherever possible, she approached local farmers with derelict farmhouses that had antique French tile roofs that were falling in, and offered to buy their tiles (originally imported from Marseilles in the 1880s as ballast for ships) at fair prices. She also used reclaimed floor tiles and wood beams, old doors, original stonework, ironwork, etc., to ensure green construction practices. These used materials were not highly valued at the time and they saved considerable money in their reclamation. Furthermore, she furnished the main house and guest suites with antiques that wealthy families were selling as a means to make ends meet.

"Today, labor costs are quite high, as are building materials. Antiques such as I found are in short supply and very highly prized. It is likely that we would not be able to afford today what we've accomplished over the past seven years. Nor would we be able to find the old tiles, stonework, etc., that have since been gobbled up."

When I asked Karen how she made the Inn financially viable she summed it up using the age-old investment strategy: diversify.

"I originally had no intention of running a guest ranch, so for the first few years we sought to make the ranch pay for itself by farming and cattle and sheep ranching. We invested in a large flock of sheep which supply both wool and lambs that we sell. The sheep are strictly grazers and require no supplemental feed; our only expense is the nominal veterinarian bills. We invested in beef cattle which provide additional profit. We farm our own alfalfa and oats to feed the horses, pigs, and cattle and also sell much of our production to other local farmers and ranchers who specialize in only one type of crop or in grazing only. Finally, we lease out some of our property to other farmers and ranchers who are able to invest the time in working the fields but are not able to invest money into land of their own.

"During the first two years I operated the Inn, we exceeded all my expectations in sales. However, with the recession we now find in Uruguay (as in the U.S.) that tourist traffic has dropped substantially. The ranch operations (i.e., the sheep, cattle, crops and leases) are currently off-setting my expenses in running the Inn, so I can still run the entire operation at a profit."

Using Life's Twists and Turns

Karen lives in Uruguay for seven months out of the year, tending to her crops, animals and the Inn. A full-time Ranch Manager runs the farm and animal operation year-round. Karen is truly rooted in the land and much of what is consumed at the Inn is grown on-site including organic lamb, beef, honey, fruit and vegetables. The wool is sold to a local cooperative and they farm their own alfalfa and oats for the horses, pigs, sheep, goats and cattle.

While she never dreamed of being a rancher and Innkeeper, let alone in Uruguay, Karen admits that life's twists and turns often provide the opportunities that are most rewarding. It's not easy and she has to make sacrifices, including the long-term separation from loved ones but she is thriving. Her ultimate goal is to add value to the business by selling and marketing farm products, textiles and hand-dyed wool.

A Mighty List of Transferable Skills:

Hospitality: While in college and shortly thereafter, Karen worked for four high-end hotels, all of which trained her how to welcome and receive guests with warmth, humor, and graciousness. She learned to cook at the side of world-renowned chef Jean-Louis Palladin, and she now uses these skills every day as she plan menus, oversees her cooks and chef, chooses wines to accompany meals, and budgets for food costs. She learned efficiency in maintaining scrupulously spotless guest rooms; she learned to accommodate strange requests with aplomb; and most importantly, she learned to always maintain a sense of humor.

Sales, Marketing and PR: Her undergraduate degree in Journalism and Public Relations led to her second career in broadcast media sales and marketing. The skills Karen learned in this field are, of course, critical in promoting one's business, although not necessarily by the business owner herself. Many entrepreneurs spend thousands of dollars hiring specialists in marketing, advertising, and PR; she has been fortunate to be able to do much of this crucial work herself.

Textile Design: Earning a Master's Degree in design honed her eye and enabled her to see the work of art in a derelict, falling down 1830s farm house inhabited by mice and rats.

> "I saw the bones of the house and had the confidence and skill (both of which I learned in design school) to renovate while keeping the architectural integrity of the building intact. Applying a critical eye to the blending of architectural styles, decorating, and landscaping ensured a thoughtful, harmonious, and beautiful outcome for the entire property."

Remember The Red Light Green Light Rule

> So what does she know now that she wishes she knew then?

> "I would have bought much, much, more property to increase our holdings and venture out into other farming and ranching practices. Otherwise, I would not change a thing in the overall picture. Of course, I was not a farmer or rancher when we began this venture, and I have made plenty of mistakes along the way like planting the wrong crops at the wrong time, trying to specialize in breeds that didn't do well in our climate, etc. These were learning experiences that have been invaluable. Oh, and perhaps I would have studied Spanish more rigorously and thoroughly!"

Karen shared some amazing advice she calls her *Red Light/Green Light* rule. She says tenacity can be overrated and we need to listen to ourselves and be perceptive. Her axiom is that multiple red lights might mean that you are on the wrong road. "Look for the green lights and play to your strengths by showcasing what you do well. Don't beat yourself up by trying to get through the proverbial red light. The green light road is easier for a reason – enjoy this journey, it will be better for you in the long run."

Karen's Advice and Action Steps:

- Be open to accept a new opportunity when it presents itself.
- What you learned in school should not limit what you do in life.
- Use your interests as a point of departure.
- Consider bartering or trading for services and products within your network.
- You have to love what you are doing to make your business work.

Resources:

Estancia Tierra Santa: www.estanciatierrasanta.com
Savor the Success: www.savorthesuccess.com
Ladies Who Launch: www.ladieswholaunch.com

"Life takes twists and turns, sometimes serendipity and the things we least expect are the opportunities that are most rewarding."

– Karen Vandergrift

ᔑ ᔑ ᔑ ᔑ

50. CAROL COVIN: A CURE FOR CANCER IN HER DESK

For 25 years Carol Covin enjoyed a career in the computer industry as a software engineer, but in 1997 something significant happened that would change the course of her career dramatically. Carol's colleague, with inoperable stomach cancer, found an obscure cancer treatment developed by a scientist in the late 1970s. It was held by a private scientific library the scientist endowed to hold his papers before he died in 1986. Carol's friend followed the scientist's suggested cancer treatment protocol and his 30-pound tumor was gone in six weeks.

Her friend handed Carol a copy of the protocol and said "This works – I am living proof!" His concern was that it would never be patented because it was all natural and he feared that it would never make it to clinical trials due to lack of funding and serious interest by the medical community. Carol's friend died shortly afterwards of liver damage sustained during the five-year growth of his tumor but his body was cancer free.

Clean out Your Junk Drawer

The cancer treatment protocol remained in Carol's desk for seven years while her career took several different turns. Carol quit the computer company where she had worked for eight years and started a publishing company and flourished, publishing her sixth book with her new company following five others with a previous publisher. But the cancer protocol sitting in her desk drawer kept haunting her and eventually prompted her to seek out the scientific library where the protocol was archived. Carol is quick to point out that she is not a doctor or a scientist but she got so involved in the research, she started telling people that she was working on a cure for cancer. Nobody laughed, and many offered to help.

Eventually the networking stars aligned and Carol was introduced to a pediatric oncologist, who used to work at the FDA, the NCI, and a major pharmaceutical company. She was experienced in fraud detection and interested in alternative treatments and has been guiding Carol's research ever since. Today Carol is incorporated and the President of her own company: **Sky Blue Pharmaceuticals, LLC.** She is seeking funding to conduct a Phase I clinical trial for the cancer treatment protocol.

A Sense of Urgency

It's not often that you meet someone working on a cure for cancer. I asked Carol if she was excited to get up every morning to work on this profound new career path and she said that she is extremely focused but also feels a sense of urgency to accomplish her goal.

"I went to a memorial service last summer for a friend's daughter. She died after her breast cancer recurred. I was reacquainted with her two high school children – their mom had baby-sat for my younger son. I left with a renewed sense of urgency to make this cancer treatment protocol a reality."

Everyone knows someone who has been affected by cancer. According to the National Institutes of Health, five hundred sixty-two thousand deaths from cancer were projected for 2009. Every minute, of every hour, of every day, someone will die of cancer and Carol Covin is on a mission to cut that number down considerably, knowing the ones she misses will be somebody's loved ones.

Identify Your Purpose in Life

The mission to cure cancer sounds noble but how does a non-scientist even begin to tackle this herculean task? Initially, Carol set aside $5,000 from money she inherited from her mother to hire a consultant to assess her scientific literature review. Carol had gone to the National Library of Medicine on the campus of the National Institutes of Health (NIH) to gather information that had already been written on this topic and read the citations of those sources to educate herself and others on this approach.

Her goal is to find out if the treatment works and if it does, to tell people about it. Ultimately she wants to take the treatment to market. But before she can do any of this she must take the protocol through clinical trials, to prove the claim that it has some effect on cancer.

The **Sky Blue Pharmaceuticals** team of two includes Carol and the pediatric oncologist who is guiding her research efforts. Carol has not yet had access to grants so she is relying on private funding, and clinical trials are not cheap. Ultimately, she hopes a pharmaceutical company will offer to license her product and take it to market; but the Phase I, and possibly Phase II clinical trials must happen first.

Trials and Tribulations

The cancer treatment protocol will be taken by the patient in the form of a pill on a 30-day regimen. It takes about three to six months to manufacture the pill and the full Phase I clinical trial will take about a year with 1 to 2 months of treatment and then observation, and follow-up testing. The recipe and production of the protocol will cost approximately five hundred thousand dollars and another three million dollars to facilitate the clinical trial.

Carol has a business plan and a line item budget and she is looking for investors to help underwrite the cost of the clinical trial. Venture capitalists will be pitched after the trials, so for now, she is living off her 401K which looks more like a 201K in the current economy.

She is networking like mad, connecting with entrepreneurs and women's business organizations as well as people who are living with cancer. **Sky Blue Pharmaceuticals** is truly a labor of love since there is no money coming in for Carol, but she considers this her full-time career and she is committed to meeting her goal of bringing this protocol to market.

Carol has learned that you need to identify what you need and then ask for it. This was a lesson that took a while to sink in, but Carol can say with confidence now that her life has purpose and she is unflappable in the face of adversity.

Assembling a resource team was crucial for Carol and she works with a team of advisors who are helping her make the clinical trial goal a reality. She is learning the art of fundraising and is perfecting the subtleties of "the ask" since at the end of the day, what she needs most is financial support.

Seek and You Will Find

Research has become one of Carol's top transferable skills these days. She found an online message board and unearthed discussions among people who had tried the protocol. She posted a message to ask if they were willing to be interviewed about their experience, and, if possible, supply supporting medical documentation. This has resulted in 15 case studies, including seven who supplied medical documentation, from people who had actually utilized the protocol successfully to treat their cancerous tumors. This information is now documented in a brief that will be part of the clinical trial application.

This particular protocol is unique because it is a treatment for cancerous tumors and not a preventive measure. But preparing for government application for a clinical trial has been a lesson in patience and perseverance. Carol has a 50-year plan for the rest of her life that she breaks down into 10-year chunks. She predicts it will take 8 to 10 years to get the protocol to market and she is in it for the long haul.

No One Else is Going to Do It

In the last nine months, Carol has added another advisor to her team and is talking with a law firm about a promising road map to a patent. She also won the STEM Award (Science, Technology, Engineering and Math) for a case study called The Hot Mommas Project. Carol submitted the study to George Washington University's Business School and presented a poster on the project at the Annual 2010 Multinational Development for Women in Technology (MD-WIT) conference.

Nobody expects a software engineer to cure cancer but Carol has taken this on as a personal mission. She has always put herself into challenging situations and thrives on intellectual stimulation. While some people are dubious about her efforts to cure cancer, more are applauding her and sharing personal stories of people in their lives affected by cancer. These connections have offered Carol hope and inspiration to tackle the monumental challenge she has dedicated her life to pursue.

Blue Skies

Carol left the security of a steady career to pursue a very risky venture because it speaks to her heart. Many years ago, her husband had a cancer scare but he is alive and well today; Carol lost a former college roommate to cancer, who left behind three young children; there are countless others who have been robbed of life by this selfish disease, including the colleague who gave her the business-launching protocol.

When someone asks Carol Covin at a cocktail party, "What do you do for a living?" – she answers with confidence, "I am working on a cure for cancer!" And she really means it.

Carol's Advice and Action Steps:

- Reflect on how you want to make a difference in the world. What is the imprint you will leave?
- Look to the end goal and keep your eye on the prize.
- Assemble a great team early in your venture.

Resources:

The Hot Mommas Project: Case Study. "No One Else Is Going to Do It." STEM Award 2010: www.hotmommasproject.org/caseview/Carol-L--Covin-Sky-Blue-Pharmaceuticals,-LLC-No-One-Else-Is-Going-To-Do-It.aspx

The Hot Momma's Award Presentation, GWU School of Business: www.slideshare.net/HotMommasProject/2010-awardspresentation-hotmommasproject

❝Identify what you need and then ask for it!❞

– Carol Covin

ⱷ ⱷ ⱷ ⱷ

51. Take a Step Forward

We spend nearly half our lives and most of our waking hours in the workplace. So we owe it to ourselves to create enriching experiences during those hours that are meaningful and gratifying. Jacqueline Edelberg, Anne Shroeder, Karen Vandergrift, and Carol Covin are committed to careers that bring them joy and help others in the process. Some of these opportunities came unexpectedly and others were carefully planned; but all these career reinventions happened because these women were willing to try something new.

Tapping Your Inner Indiana Jones

Say yes more often and be willing to explore new things at work. Many people discover their calling by the moves they make at work. If you are open to new experiences, assignments, projects, travel, and training, for example – you just might find something you love to do that you are very good at that was previously unknown to you. By saying yes to new things passionately you will show your boss that you are the go-to person to be counted on and this could lead to new opportunities.

I have always been willing to take a risk and have tried many new things beyond my operatic career. By trial and error I was able to determine what I really loved and what I wanted to spend more time and energy pursuing. I have many more things on my future career wish list that I am eager to try in the near future.

Jacqueline and the Roscoe Park moms took a risk trying to rehabilitate Nettlehorst School. Their gamble paid off and now this school serves as a model and inspiration for the neighborhood school renaissance movement across the nation. Taking a risk can often lead to a reward, but you will never know if you don't try.

Don't be Afraid to Fail

Experiencing failure is a reality for each of us in our careers. Some employers won't hire you, others won't promote you, and some dream jobs will be disappointing. Congratulations – welcome to the human race. We are all fallible and once you have experienced failure, you will be better at knowing how to recover the next time around.

Failure can be painful, but we learn valuable lessons when things don't go as planned. The real failure comes from never trying something in the first place. In the moving words of author and journalist, Gail Sheehy:

"If we don't change, we don't grow.

If we don't grow, we are not really living.

Growth demands a temporary surrender of security."

Show Your Enthusiasm

I can say with humility and appreciation that I have been recruited for many positions throughout my professional life. I take pride in doing my job to the best of my ability and I always try to show a genuine enthusiasm and sincere interest in taking the job above and beyond the call of duty. Perhaps ambition is in my DNA. I have a strong work ethic that gives me great satisfaction in doing a job well and overcoming challenges. This has served me well, as others have recognized my competencies and invited me to take advantage of new careers that they believed would be a good fit.

Be cognizant of the fact that other people with hiring authority may poach you away for a new career, and that can be a very exciting thing. Don't be a well-kept secret in your job success. Perform to the best of your abilities and let others know that you are open to new adventures!

The Barter and Trade System

You may have a tremendous skill that is in great demand from others, and likewise you may have friends and colleagues with an expertise you need but don't have in your personal toolbox. Consider the barter or trade system to swap what you have for what you need.

Let's say you are interested in creating a website for a freelance business that could turn your hobby into a full-time career if it takes off. You have a graphic design background and can create images and a logo for the business but you need a web programmer to create the technical foundation for the site and a copywriter to help you flesh out the written content. Look to your network to see if you can swap services with someone else who needs something you do well.

Swapping goes back for centuries as a way to make payment for services rendered. Now you can tap into the vast internet network for online swapping sites like BarterQuest.com, SwapTree.com, and Swap.net to find people who have exactly what you need for an equally measured swap.

Don't Be Limited by Your Education

Many people fear pursuing a career change because they don't have a degree in what they believe is the requisite field. Except for some very specialized fields, such as medicine and law, many careers rely more on your transferable skills, your willingness to learn, and your emotional intelligence than your degree qualifications.

Did you know that Mick Jagger was an Economics major at the rigorous London School of Economics before becoming an iconic rock star? Michelle Obama studied sociology and African-American studies at Princeton University before heading to Harvard Law.

They each developed core skills and a specific knowledge base from their respective disciplines, but these high profile individuals went on to develop careers that were not limited to the academic choices they made in school.

REINVENTION TOOLBOX

Using a Coach – Best Practices; Honor Your Self

Olympians and professional athletes at the top of their game have been utilizing coaches for decades so why is it that professionals in the world-of-work have taken so long to catch up? A coach stands on the sidelines and gives you input and objectivity that you cannot effectively produce yourself. You should hire a coach because you want to get better at what you are already good at.

A good coach will help you discover what you need and will provide you with a strategic action plan, motivation, and accountability to accomplish your goals. While change in the workplace is inevitable, suffering is optional; a coach can help you unlock what you are passionate about and help you move forward if you are contemplating a career transition or professional reinvention.

Coaches can provide you with opportunities to own your self-confidence and play to your strengths. A great coach once told me that individuals bloom when they decide to ride their horse in the direction it is already going.

Are Your Coachable?

Shop wisely for a coach and be aware that the industry standard is to provide a free consultation to learn about their services and to determine if it's a good fit for you. Use your intuitive and perceptive senses to gut-check whether a prospective coach is a good match for what you need. This is an investment in your career and your life, so look for someone you can trust, that comes well recommended (check references), and provides a complimentary consultation so that you can get to know each other before you sign up.

Coaches specialize in a wide variety of services, including personal branding, executive development, communications, entrepreneurial ventures, social media, and leadership enhancement, to name just a few. Be sure to find a coach that specializes in what you need most. There is a niche market ripe with coaches dedicated to all areas of expertise. Find one who is a specialist and not a Jack-of-all-trades to get the most focused coaching experience possible.

If you are considering the services of a coach, I am happy to help get you started on your quest for the best fit. Please contact me through my website www.carolinedowdhiggins. com.

A Lesson from Tracy Robbins

Jane Austen, the English novelist was known for her biting social commentary in the 1800s. I believe she would have been an avid blogger if she was alive today with hundreds of connections in her LinkedIn profile. As much as I adore Jane Austen's work, whenever I re-read her novels or watch a movie or mini-series, it makes me appreciate the modern times in which I live.

Jane's plots, although often comedic, highlight the dependence of women on marriage to secure social standing and economic security. She was a rare bird to be a female published author in her day. Thankfully, times have changed and modern women can make their way in the world, with or without a significant other in their lives. Women today have choices and have been empowered to lead authentic lives and forge careers that are meaningful to us as individuals.

Jane Austen would have been inspired by Tracy Robbins, the highest ranking woman and Executive Vice President of Global Human Resources for Intercontinental Hotels Group, PLC. In an interview with Pink Magazine, Tracy shared four tips for honoring yourself and finding success.

Stretch Yourself – take on projects that have potential to make a big impact on your career and your life. Make those accomplishments visible and find authentic, effective ways to promote your achievements.

Be Yourself – be genuine in your life and career choices. Don't fake it to fit in or get ahead on the job. Honoring your values and passions will reap greater rewards in the long run.

Have Fun – laughter breaks down boundaries. Add some levity to each day and don't take yourself too seriously. Develop your sense of humor and enjoy a good hearty laugh – it's good for your health.

Develop Your Team – be relentless, caring, and tenacious about developing your team. Surround yourself with great people who do what you can't and support them and encourage them to achieve success together.

11

THE FORCE OF THE SISTERHOOD

52. EMPOWERMENT, OPTIMISM, AND HUMBLE CONFIDENCE

After my own personal reinvention I feel empowered to do a great many things in my career. I believe that I have many professional lives ahead of me and I will continue to reinvent myself again and again as my values and interests change over time, and I utilize the variety of skills in my professional toolbox.

Empowerment is a buzz word in our culture that refers to increasing the spiritual, political, social, or economic strength of individuals and communities. Ideally, the empowered develop confidence in their capabilities. I am on a quest to help women own their strengths and become empowered in the workplace so that they can thrive, and can earn equal pay commensurate to their male counterparts!

The reinvention stories of these amazing women have inspired me to pay-it-forward to help women in the workforce own their strengths and gain confidence on the road to empowerment.

My friend and mentor, Deborah C. Stephens, has dealt with a lot of adversity in her life, but her positive energy is palpable and uplifting. Deborah's source of positive inspiration is her husband, Mike, who is struggling with a terminal illness. Mike has beaten the odds of the survival statistics and is hands-down, the most upbeat and optimistic person I have ever met.

A Cup Half Full

Positivity and optimism are powerful tools for us to employ daily. It's easy to focus on the negative and get depressed about what we can't control. But I urge you to be a cup half-full person and focus on what you **can** control. Celebrate that you can be the change agent for your career destiny. Positivity is infectious, so be the one in your organization who sets the tone for the work environment.

Now that you are feeling empowered and positive, let's talk about confidence. Historically, women have been taught not to brag or be boastful about their accomplishments. As a result, we are often uncomfortable promoting ourselves and we miss out on career opportunities because we don't sing our own praises in a performance review or job interview.

Practice embracing your humble confidence. This should be a blend of owning your strengths and celebrating the accomplishments you have earned and doing so in an authentic way that is professional and palatable for you and your audience.

Picture the woman in your network that walks tall with humble confidence. She owns the space she occupies in a room and she speaks with conviction. She attracts people to her with a positive energy and she is respected and well known for her accomplishments. We all know someone like this and we have great admiration for this woman in our respective networks. Think of her as a role model and channel her when you begin to put into practice your humble confidence.

53. RUNNING YOUR CAREER MARATHON

It's rare to have a single job with an organization for your entire professional career. Part of that is because work culture has changed and organizations don't incentivize company loyalty as they did years ago. Statistically, people change career fields (not just jobs) an average of 5 to 7 times during their adult lives.

Career reinvention is on the rise so you are in good company. I believe the career transition phenomenon is widespread because people are becoming more aware of what they value. They want to work in environments where they are challenged, stimulated, and gratified.

The millennial generation now entering the work force is clearly articulating that they want work/life balance. While this is unsettling for the old guard, it just may revolutionize how companies view part-time employment, flexible work schedules, work-from-home options, and longer vacation periods.

I hope the concept of the career marathon brings you comfort and helps you think of the long run in your full career life. Alma Bond is certainly not considering retirement yet and she is in her 80s. Bottom line, you always have a choice. Take stock of what mile marker you are currently at. Perhaps you are taking it slow because you are raising young children, or maybe you are ramping it up because you are eager to seek new promotional opportunities. Consider your life milestones and plan your career marathon accordingly.

54. SETTING AND ACHIEVING GOALS

Having dreams and goals for the future is a wonderful way to focus on what you want in your life and career. A wise mentor once told me it's not enough to just think about your goals – you must write them down. Putting your wishes on paper helps you articulate things more clearly and gives you accountability for achieving your goals.

Carol Covin has set out a 50-year plan for her career goal of taking a product to market that will cure cancer. Her project is massive in every respect since she must first take the cancer-curing protocol through a series of clinical trials that will literally take years to accomplish. You need not carve out a 50-year plan, but I urge you to take a close look at the next 90 days and write down what you want to accomplish. You can always change your mind and adjust your game plan, but dig deep to think about what you really want.

First, Take Baby Steps

Split your 90-day goal into smaller, attainable actions and chop it into manageable baby steps. Writing down your goals can be a secret weapon to help you focus on your objectives.

This is also a good time to look to your posse, your personal Board of Directors, or your resource team to assemble the masterminds that will help you reach your target. Identify your solutions instead of focusing on the problems; seek information and help from your advisors.

It's easy to get bogged down with over ambitious to-do lists. The point of the exercise is to manage the work flow into reasonable and attainable increments. Reaching a goal is extremely gratifying so set small, attainable goals for each day and work incrementally towards the big finale. Studies tell us that you are 90 times more likely to accomplish a goal when it is written down. What are you waiting for… grab a pen and write down your goals!

Keep Your Eye on the Prize

Once you visualize your bigger career goals, keep the focus and reward yourself for all the accomplishments you achieve along the way. Celebrate small milestones like increasing your network, pursuing informational interviews, or taking on a new assignment at work. You must reward your successes to motivate yourself to reach the end goal. Have someone on your resource team be your accountability master to hold your feet to the fire for deadlines and difficult tasks in your career plan. This person could be a friend, mentor, or a coach who can really give you the push you need to move forward, especially when times are tough.

Opportunity knocks when we least expect it so always be at-the-ready to consider and take advantage of new breaks. If you can seize the moment and come to the rescue for a difficult challenge at work – you just might be the next go-to person when it comes time for a promotion. Being well prepared is a skill in and of itself.

55. Work/life Balance and Making Choices

One of the most common questions from my students is: *How will I maintain work/life balance if I land a competitive job in the cutting edge corporate world?* I can honestly report that most of those organizations are not hiring entry-level associates and paying them mega salaries so they can enjoy work/life balance. They feed you breakfast, lunch and dinner at the office, not because it's a perk, but because they don't want you to leave the building!

You must have realistic expectations about what you value and what it requires in your work environment. I'm not saying that if you make a lot of money you won't ever have work/life balance, but I am saying that you will have to work very long hours to earn that jumbo pay check.

It's really all about making choices and looking for careers and organizations that honor what you value. If work/life balance is important to you because you want to spend time with your family, then look for companies and careers that celebrate those values.

You can have it all but it might not be all at the same time. Many of the women in this book left a corporate environment because they wanted to be more in control of their own time. The entrepreneurs love being their own boss but they know that often it takes 24/7 work to get everything done – especially for a start-up business. You can design your life around your job or design your job around your life. Neither is better or worse – but it is **your** choice.

56. CELEBRATE THE NEW YOU: RECHARGED, REIGNITED AND REINVENTED

Since we spend over half our lives in the workplace, we owe it to ourselves to be happy in our careers. We should create enriching experiences that stimulate and challenge us. I urge you to consider at least one thing you can do TODAY to turn the career you didn't order into one that you love.

Thank you for coming on this career reinvention journey with me and the women showcased in this book. The blog continues to feature women who have transitioned and reinvented, so I hope you will use that as an additional resource: www.notthecareeriordered.com.

I have learned so much from these amazing women and I am inspired by their courage, their strength, and their passion for life. Whether you are recharging and reigniting an existing career with some new strategies or reinventing yourself entirely, you have the power to do great things. Be sure to share your reinvention stories with me and perhaps I will feature you on the blog or in my next book.

My offer remains to help you with your individual career transition goals. I have dedicated my career to helping others own their strengths and embrace their confidence. You can learn more at www.carolinedowdhiggins.com – I hope to hear from you!

In addition to the resources suggested by the women featured in this book, I have included a list of some of my favorite books and websites that you may also find helpful on your career development journey.

RESOURCES

1. This Is Not the Career I Ordered – blog www.notthecareeriordered.com

2. *Now, Discover Your Strengths* by Marcus Buckingham and Donald O. Clifton

3. *The One Thing You Need to Know: ... About Great Managing, Great Leading, and Sustained Individual Success* by Marcus Buckingham

4. *Brag!: The Art of Tooting Your Own Horn without Blowing It* by Peggy Klaus

5. *The Hard Truth About Soft Skills: Workplace Lessons Smart People Wish They'd Learned Sooner* by Peggy Klaus

6. *See Jane Lead: 99 Ways for Women to Take Charge at Work* by Lois P. Frankel

7. *This Is Not the Life I Ordered: 50 Ways to Keep Your Head Above Water When Life Keeps Dragging You Down* by Deborah Collins Stephens, Michealene Cristini Risley, Jackie Speier, and Jan Yanehiro

8. *On Becoming Fearless...In Love, Work and Life* by Arianna Huffington

9. *What Color is Your Parachute?* by Richard N. Bolles

10. *Knock 'em Dead – The Ultimate Job Search Guide 2010* by Martin Yate

11. *The Art of Dialogue* by Carolyn Zeisset

12. *Do What You Are* by Paul D. Tieger and Barbara Barron-Tieger

13. *The Fine Art of Small Talk: How to Start a Conversation, Keep it Going, Build Rapport and Leave a Positive Impression* by Debra Fine

14. *The Fine Art of the Big Talk: How to Win Clients, Deliver Great Presentations, and Solve Conflicts at Work* by Debra Fine

15. *GRADS: TAKE CHARGE of Your First Year After College!* by Kathryn Marion

16. The Practical Mentor – Paul Marrangoni: www.practicalmentor.com

17. Dr. Mildred C. Culp – Workwise: www.workwise.net/

18. The Wage Project: www.wageproject.org/

19. Myers-Briggs Foundation: www.myersbriggs.org

20. Strong Interest Inventory at CPP: www.cpp.com/products/strong/index.aspx

21. CPP The Development People: www.cpp.com/en/index.aspx

22. Savor the Success: www.savorthesuccess.com

23. 85 Broads: www.85broads.com

24. Fearless Women Network, Starla Sireno – Founder, CEO: www.FearlessWomenNetwork.com

ABOUT THE AUTHOR

With over a decade of career and professional development coaching experience, Caroline Dowd-Higgins has a desire to empower and energize people to achieve their personal goals. Her training style is engaging, high energy, and positive with a focus on unlocking the self-advocate within each of us.

In her capacity as a Director of Career and Professional Development at the Indiana University Maurer School of Law, she prepares the next generation of lawyers to be ready for the career world. Working nationally with employers and alumni to find and develop new jobs for law students, she has become an expert in mining new opportunities that showcase the value of transferable skills.

A regular blogger for the *Huffington Post* online, Caroline focuses on career and professional development topics and also pens a monthly column for *The Chronicle* newspaper in Northern Indiana. Her articles have been picked up for international distribution and she is a sought after talk radio guest for career themed broadcasts. She also serves on the Conference Advisory Board for Invent Your Future, Inc.

An accomplished public speaker, Caroline is a member of the National Speaker's Association and enjoys presenting to audiences across the nation. She is adept at helping individuals fine tune their communication skills to improve their professional public image and effectiveness in the workplace. A frequent workshop facilitator for corporate and nonprofit entities, Caroline enjoys personal coaching and group sessions to help maximize communication effectiveness, on-the-job performance, and career satisfaction.

Her formal education includes a Bachelor's and Master's degree in Music from the Indiana University Jacobs School of Music. Her many years singing on the professional stage have helped her hone the fine art of self-promotion and stage presence. She has significant experience working with college students helping them transition from academia into the world-of-work and she also enjoys working with a diverse clientele of all ages and backgrounds in her private practice.

As a testimony to the power of transferable skills, prior to establishing her consulting practice, Caroline worked as a professional opera singer in Europe and the United States. She has also appeared in a myriad of commercials, voice-over spots, industrial films and live theatrical productions as a featured actress.

Caroline's goal is to empower women, so it's unsurprising that her first book, *This Is Not the Career I Ordered*, focuses on women who have experienced a career transition and reinvented themselves in the job world. The book and blog of the same name serve as a resource and an inspiration for women who have survived a career change brought about by choice or necessity. Caroline's goal is to provide empowering strategies and action steps to help others move forward.

CPSIA information can be obtained at www.ICGtesting.com
Printed in the USA
LVOW101257290413

331289LV00001B/2/P